Don't Call Me Gypsy

Don't Call Me Gypsy

A Journey through Czech Romani
History and Fairy Tales

Kytka Hilmarová

CZECH REVIVAL
PUBLISHING

Czech Revival Publishing.
www.czechrevival.com
US+ 727-238-7884

The views expressed in this work are solely those of the author and do not necessarily reflect the opinions or policies of any organization or individual. The author's personal experiences and opinions are shared for the purposes of entertainment and education. The reader should form their own conclusions and opinions based on the content presented, and the author assumes no responsibility for any actions taken by the reader as a result. Any references made to people, organizations, or events are based on the author's recollection and interpretation and may not be entirely accurate or comprehensive. This work is not intended to provide legal, financial, or professional advice, and the author recommends that readers consult with qualified professionals in these areas before making any decisions.

Book Design, Formatting, and Cover by Kytka Hilmarová

Library of Congress Cataloging-in-Publication Data

Hilmarova, Kytka 1964-
        Don't Call Me Gypsy : A Journey through Czech Romani History and Fairy Tales / Kytka Hilmarová

Summary: Don't Call Me Gypsy: A Journey through Czech Romani History and Fairy Tales is a transformative exploration of the Romani community's history, culture, and resilience. Through their nomadic lifestyle, triumph over oppression, vibrant cultural expressions, and enchanting fairytales, this book celebrates their enduring strength and calls for empathy and understanding. – Provided by publisher.

ISBN 13: 978-1-943103-25-6

1. Anthropology. 2. Roma People, Gypsies. 3. Folklore 4. Fairy Tales

Na daran Romale vi
ame sam Rom chache

Do not fear, you Gypsy men,
for we too, are Gypsies.

Contents

Acknowledgments

I would like to express my heartfelt gratitude to my beloved Babička, Marie Hilmarová (born Šrámková, December 5, 1923 - November 12, 2005), whose Austrian royalty combined with vibrant Romani spirit inspired and ignited us all. Your love and guidance continue to shape my journey.

I am immensely grateful to Anna and Milan Hilmar for their unwavering support, encouragement, and unwavering belief in me. Your presence and belief in my work have been instrumental in my pursuit of this book.

To Zachary, Zanna, and Zynnia, you are my anchor, my sanctuary, and my home no matter where my path leads. Your love and understanding have been a constant source of strength and inspiration.

Introduction

In order to provide a comprehensive exploration, it is crucial to acknowledge the historical context surrounding the terminology employed to refer to the Romani people. While the term "gypsy" has been historically used, it is currently deemed offensive by many within the Romani community. This term perpetuates stereotypes and has been utilized as a means of marginalization and discrimination. Instead, it is recommended to employ terms such as "Romani," "Romany," or "Roma" to accurately represent their identity and demonstrate respect for their cultural heritage.

Throughout this book, various terminologies, including "gypsy," are utilized, particularly in the section dedicated to the fairy tales.

Tracing their presence back several centuries, the Romani people's history in the Czech lands can be ascertained through historical records that document their arrival as early as the 14th century. Over time, this community has undergone transformations, carving out distinct traditions, customs, and dialects within the Czech Republic. From rural settlements to nomadic trade routes, their journey has been shaped by the vicissitudes of history. Nestled within the Czech Republic, they constitute an ethnic minority group with a heritage deeply rooted in Romani culture. Possessing a unique language, traditions, and a captivating history spanning across Europe, they have indelibly influenced the fabric of Czech society.

The initial segment of this book offers a concise history of the Romani people in Czechoslovakia. Similar to numerous other communities, the Romani people have encountered social, economic, and political challenges throughout their extensive history. Discrimination, marginalization, and social exclusion have cast shadows over their lives, hindering their access to education, employment, healthcare, and fundamental rights. Nevertheless, amid these obstacles, the Romani people have demonstrated remarkable resilience, emerging as beacons of strength and perseverance.

Within the Czech Republic, diverse subgroups and regional variations exist among the larger Romani population, each contributing unique perspectives, traditions, and experiences. Despite their adversities, many individuals of Romani descent have made significant contributions to various domains, including arts, music, literature, and advocacy for Romani rights and culture. Their presence enriches the tapestry of Czech society, interweaving a diverse and vibrant nation. Efforts to preserve and promote Romani culture and heritage are underway, with initiatives dedicated to documenting and reviving traditional Romani folklore, music, and language. Romani festivals, cultural events, and organizations play a pivotal role in celebrating and sharing the richness of Romani traditions with the broader Czech society, fostering a deeper comprehension and appreciation for their vibrant cultural legacy.

The second part of this book delves into twelve gypsy fairy tales. These tales are sourced from a book I have translated, entitled *Cikánské Pohádky*, originally published in

1913 by A.L. Hynek and translated by Zdenka Hostinska. The Czech translator drew material from the works of Dr. H. Von Wlislocki dating back to 1886. The original author recounted that during his travels with the Romani people, they shared these ancient tales while seated beside a parked caravan, illuminated by a blazing fire.

As we embark on this captivating exploration of the remarkable history and rich cultural tapestry of the Romani people in the Czech Republic, we embark on a journey of discovery, understanding, and celebration. Together, let us embrace the individuality, resilience, and contributions of the Romani community, forging a path toward a more inclusive and compassionate society that cherishes the diverse narratives of its inhabitants.

Romani in the Czech Lands

The Gypsies

The historical journey of the Roma people is a tapestry woven with complex threads of societal perceptions and assimilation attempts. As they settled in various parts of Europe, their experiences were shaped by a diverse range of acceptance and resistance. From enduring expulsion and persecution to facing forced assimilation and restrictive mandates, the Roma community has confronted formidable challenges in their quest for recognition and integration into European societies.

Throughout their migratory path across different regions of Europe, the Roma encountered a multitude of designations and labels that reflected the evolving perceptions and interactions with the majority of the populations. These terms offer insights into the intricate history and cultural heritage of the Roma community, shedding light on the complexities of their identity and societal relationships.

Historical sources often portrayed the Roma as outlaws, subjecting them to expulsion and persecution. Their presence was deemed illegal in the majority of Christian Europe, establishing a persistent barrier before and after their settlement in various regions.

During their arrival in Byzantium, the Roma were mistakenly associated with the term "gypsy." This misidentification arose from their perceived resemblance to another group known as the "Acingans." Both the Roma and the Acingans were believed to possess mystical powers and were associated with practices of white and dark magic. These arcane traditions were considered perilous and were even linked to satanic forces during that era. Interestingly, the Roma's mystical

6

practices, such as spells and divination, were thought to provide protection to a Byzantine king during his hunting expeditions. Consequently, Byzantine church authorities repeatedly cautioned their followers about the Acingans/Cingans, viewing them as individuals who had forged pacts with the devil. As a result, the term "gypsy" acquired a negative connotation during the deep Middle Ages.

In the 15th century, another designation gained prominence: the belief in the Roma's Egyptian origin. This perception stemmed from their nomadic lifestyle and physical features, which some observers associated with the ancient Egyptians. However, it is important to note that this belief in their Egyptian heritage is not supported by historical evidence.

The circulation of a legend among both the public and professionals played a significant role in the widespread use of terms like "gypsy" in English or "gitano" in Spanish, which derive from the word "Egypt." According to Christian folklore, the Roma were believed to have originated from Egypt but had deviated from the Christian faith following the arrival of Muslim Turks.

However, they expressed a deep longing to return to their Christian roots. As a form of penance, they were condemned to a nomadic existence, perpetually wandering the world without a true homeland. This legend, with its various interpretations, aimed to convey to Europeans that although the Roma had made mistakes, they were actively seeking redemption and a renewed connection with the Christian faith.

As a result, the term "gypsy" no longer carries the same negative connotations as it did in the past and is met with less reservation by the Roma community today compared to a decade ago.

In the 16th and particularly the 17th and 18th centuries, the Roma people experienced a period marked by numerous potentially interconnected factors that plunged them into a state of marginalization and persecution. Europe viewed the Roma as unwanted outcasts due to their distinctive appearance, unfamiliar culture, loose religious affiliations, the pervasive and irrational confusion between Roma and Turks, and the perception of their parasitic existence within the majority society. Official documents in most European countries, excluding the Ottoman Empire, repeatedly prohibited their presence.

The consequences for defying these prohibitions grew increasingly severe, even for those who sought to assist the Roma. Antigypsy decrees referred to members of Roma groups as wanderers or vagabonds, implying that individuals without such identities would not face fatal consequences. However, Roma individuals identified as part of the group or independently but exhibiting Roma traits often endured harsh trials and public executions as a deterrent. Those spared from execution, often women and children during initial capture, were forcibly escorted to the country's borders by the military, where they were compelled to sign a document pledging not to return.

In the southern realms, particularly in the parts of Europe dominated by the Ottoman Empire, the Roma encountered fewer hindrances. Hungary, for instance, witnessed Roma settlements as early as the 15th and 16th centuries, while the 18th century saw further progress aided by the Teresian assimilation and sedentarization project. These endeavors facilitated a more settled existence for the

Roma within Hungarian society, offering them opportunities for integration and stability.

Assimilation and Sedentarization

The Teresian assimilation and sedentarization project denotes a historical initiative that unfolded during the reign of Empress Maria Theresa of Austria (1740-1780). This project aimed to effect societal and cultural transformations within the Romani population, specifically targeting their integration into the dominant social fabric and discouraging their distinct nomadic way of life.

Through various means, such as enforced settlements, restrictions on traditional occupations, and the promotion of settled habits, the Teresian assimilation and sedentarization project sought to bring about substantial changes among the Roma. The intention was to improve their social and economic conditions by facilitating their assimilation into mainstream society.

This ambitious undertaking left a profound impact on the Romani community, reshaping their living arrangements, economic activities, and cultural traditions. While the project sought to ameliorate the circumstances of the

Romani population, it also entailed the loss of their traditional nomadic lifestyle and the erosion of their cultural heritage. It is worth noting that Spain similarly imposed compulsory settlement measures upon the Roma, particularly during the infamous Great Anti-Gypsy Raid in the mid-18th century.

The Great Anti-Gypsy Raid

The Great Anti-Gypsy Raid, which occurred in the mid-18th century, signifies a significant series of coordinated actions aimed at the Romani population across various European countries during that period. These actions were characterized by organized raids, persecutions, and mass expulsions specifically targeting Romani communities.

The underlying motivations behind these raids stemmed from deeply ingrained prejudice, stereotypes, and misconceptions surrounding the Romani people. They were often driven by a perceived need to maintain social order, safeguard economic interests, and eliminate what was erroneously perceived as a threat to established societal norms.

During the course of the Great Anti-Gypsy Raid, Romani individuals and families faced forceful eviction from their homes, confiscation of their belongings, and frequent instances of physical violence and discrimination. The consequences of these raids resulted in the displacement and scattering of Romani communities, further marginalizing them within society.

Nevertheless, it is important to note that some Roma communities have managed to maintain their nomadic way of life in countries such as France and Britain. Despite historical pressures to assimilate and settle, these communities have successfully preserved their traditional practices characterized by mobility and a profound connection to their cultural heritage.

For instance, in France, certain Roma groups continue to live in caravans, traveling from one location to another while engaging in their traditional crafts and trades. They face ongoing challenges in finding suitable camping sites and accessing basic services, yet they persist in upholding their nomadic identity.

Similarly, in Britain, select Roma communities choose to reside in caravans or trailers, periodically moving to different areas in search of seasonal employment or improved living conditions. Throughout their journey, they steadfastly uphold their unique traditions, language, and cultural practices, navigating the complexities of modern society while retaining their distinct way of life.

Circling Nomads

During an era characterized by widespread persecution and the nomadic trajectory of the Roma across Europe, a remarkable sense of solidarity and mutual understanding emerged among members of various Roma groups. This unity was forged through their shared experience of marginalization on the periphery of society.

Paradoxically, the distancing of themselves from an unsupportive and hostile majority became a defining moment that either strengthened or contributed to the formation of Romani identity. The majority's aversion towards "gypsies" led to two opposing tendencies that persist to this day. On one hand, there is a desire to deny their origins and disassociate from the despised and stigmatized ethnicity, which is primarily manifested externally. On the other hand, there is an internal and subtle unification and support for a shared identity based on rejection by the majority, which is more prevalent within the community itself.

Defining the Roma people has always posed a complex challenge. Today, Roma communities are dispersed globally, with an estimated population of 8 to 12 million residing in Europe alone. Despite their geographical diversity, the Roma engage with their surrounding regions and inhabitants in distinctive ways, fostering intercultural exchanges and embracing diverse customs.

These interactions have given rise to the proliferation of numerous dialects within the Romani language, reflecting the regional variations that have evolved over time. For instance, in Slovakia, a popular saying encapsulates the diversity among Roma communities: "Šel vatri – šel Roma," which translates to "One hundred settlements – a hundred times different Roma." However, in a momentous declaration made during the 5th congress of the International Romani Union held in Prague in 2000, Roma leaders affirmed their belonging to a unified Roma nation, transcending national borders and emphasizing their shared identity.

This proclamation marked a significant milestone in the international efforts to foster collaboration and unity among Roma communities, gaining momentum in the latter half of the 20th century.

Bohemia, Moravia, and Slovakia

The presence of the Romani people in the Czech lands dates back several centuries, with historical records indicating their arrival as early as the 14th century. Their migration from northern India and subsequent journeys across continents brought them to Eastern Europe, including the Czech lands. Their movement was influenced by various factors, such as economic opportunities, political upheavals, and the desire to escape persecution and discrimination.

In the historical chronicles of the Czech lands, the first documented references to the Roma people appear in Dalimil's Chronicle, a written account from the early 14th century. The last entry in this chronicle dates to the year 1314, attesting to the presence of Roma in the Czech lands during that time.

During their initial arrival, Czech society embraced the Roma with openness. The Roma, with their captivating stories and mythical narratives, were welcomed as they traversed a Europe steeped in Christian traditions, despite their own distinct cultural practices. Tales circulated, claiming that Roma blacksmiths had forged the very nails used in the crucifixion of Jesus or that they had refused shelter to Mary and Joseph during the birth of Jesus. These stories intrigued and fascinated the Christian populace, resulting in a warm reception for the Roma.

However, as the 15th century began, the Church started questioning the Roma people's adherence to Christian customs. This shift in perception led to a series of unfortunate events for the Roma across Europe. Accusations of arson and allegations of spying for the Turks further fueled the growing resentment towards the Roma. These circumstances culminated in their persecution, with acts of violence and discrimination becoming commonplace.

Historical sources reveal instances where Roma individuals captured outside their communities tried to convince the courts that they were not Roma, denying any affiliation and attributing their dark skin to summer sun exposure. Similarly, in later centuries, Roma individuals in various European countries adopted common and pleasing-sounding names, such as Růžička (Little Rose), Winter, Zima (Winter), Vrba (Willow), Janeček, and others, in an effort to mitigate discrimination.

The initial Roma settlers in the southeastern regions of Moravia benefited from the tolerance of the nobility towards their presence. This tolerance, however, came with conditions: the Roma had to sever ties with their extended families, abandon the use of the Romani language, and forsake their traditional attire. Assimilation became the prevailing mandate. Violating these regulations risked extradition to the capital court, where individuals would be tried for violating anti-Gypsy mandates and unauthorized presence in the Czech lands.

Within the Czech lands, which were divided into the Kingdom of Bohemia and the Margraviate of Moravia, the Roma faced a harsh fate. Symbolically, when a Roma individual appeared in the Margraviate of Moravia, their left ear was severed to signify their presence, while in the Czech lands, their right ear was removed. This cruel practice served as a visible reminder of the Romani status and subjected them to further mistreatment. Caught for a third time, severe punishments awaited them, including drowning, hanging, or burning.

The situation began to change with the ascension of Maria Theresa to the throne. Initially following her father's policies, she perpetuated the marginalization of the Roma. However, over time, she introduced a policy of assimilation that extended not only to the Roma but also to all Czechs. Unfortunately, while this policy may have alleviated certain forms of persecution, it also resulted in the erasure of cultural identities and the imposition of societal norms upon the Roma community.

Act No. 117

The Czech lands grappled with various challenges in their interactions with the Roma population, ranging from outright bans on their entry with severe penalties to regulations and restrictions on their movement. It was not until 1927, with the implementation of Act No. 117 and its accompanying regulations, that measures were put in place to properly register gypsy gangs. This registration allowed the gendarmerie to enhance their ability to detect and punish crimes committed by Roma individuals. However, the laws of that time did not exclusively refer to the term "gypsy" as denoting membership in a specific ethnic group. Instead, it encompassed individuals who lived according to the gypsy way, a term that was broadly defined and resulted in inconsistencies in law enforcement. Nevertheless, certain trades and occupations, such as bootleggers, shoemakers, grinders, and traveling jugglers, were exempted from this classification.

The Roma traveled in groups, following specific routes and settling in proximity to inhabited areas, often camping in forests to avoid immediate detection. The village mayor had to obtain permission for the Roma to camp in a designated area, with their stay limited to a predetermined period. Once the allotted time expired, the Roma would relocate to another municipality's territory to continue their temporary settlement. In order to facilitate their mobility and flexibility, Roma individuals often possessed multiple documents, including baptismal certificates, with different names. The gendarmerie played a significant role in dealing with the Roma population, exercising authority that differed significantly from that of the modern-day police force. Villages where the Roma camped faced not only issues such as begging, fortune-telling, and petty theft, but also more serious crimes, including robbery and attempted murder. Evicting Roma from buildings would often elicit concerns of retaliation, such as property arson. The recollections of former gendarmes provide valuable testimonies regarding the numerous troubles and challenges associated with gypsy gangs during that period.

Prior to World War II, two groups of Roma resided in the territory of the Czech Republic. Čeněk Růžička from the Committee for the Compensation of Romani Holocaust sheds light on their shared experiences and differences in lifestyle during that time:

"In the Czech lands, Roma have deep-rooted ties dating back 600 years, and until 1942, there were still original Czech Roma, known as 'Sinti.' These Roma originally came from Germany and lived here until 1942 when the Roma genocide occurred. The majority of them ended up in Nazi concentration camps, including the Lety camp and the concentration camp in Hodonín u Kunštátu in Moravia, which housed the Moravian Roma. Only a small fraction of the original Czech Roma and Sinti returned from the concentration camps.

During that time, some Roma individuals who possessed information believed that Slovakia, which was perceived to have a pro-fascist state, offered better chances for survival. Consequently, some of them emigrated to Slovakia. Additionally, there were opportunities to 'buy off' Roma individuals from the Protectorate. Unfortunately, certain corrupt officials in the Czech Protectorate's criminal police were susceptible to bribes.

We are aware of the amounts in gold for which a given Czech Roma or Sinto could be 'bought off' if they lacked the financial means. However, this option was limited to a small group of individuals who kept it discreet, fearing exposure and the subsequent termination of the opportunity. Consequently, families like the Růžičkas or Čermáks, among others, were unaware of this option, and the majority of them perished in the concentration camps."

Czechoslovak Romani During WWII

In 1939, the division of Czechoslovakia into the Protectorate of Bohemia and Moravia and the creation of the Slovak state, which aligned itself with Hitler's regime, had profound and devastating consequences for the Roma population. The Roma residing in Bohemia and Moravia faced a dire and uncertain fate as the dark clouds of persecution loomed over their communities. The unfolding events would leave an indelible mark on their history, causing immeasurable suffering and loss.

As the wheels of division turned, the Roma found themselves caught in the crosscurrents of political upheaval and racial discrimination. Many were forcibly uprooted from their homes, torn away from their communities, and stripped of their basic human rights. The tightening grip of Nazi ideology and the implementation of draconian policies led to the systematic persecution and marginalization of the Roma people.

Between 1941 and 1943, the wheels of oppression reached a new level of cruelty as numerous Romani individuals from Bohemia and Moravia were rounded up and transported to concentration camps. The names of these camps have become chilling symbols of human suffering and tragedy: Lety u Písek and Hodonín near Kunštát. Lety u Písek, once a place where pigs roamed, became a site of unimaginable horrors, where Romani lives were devalued and destroyed. Hodonín near Kunštát, once a place of leisure and joy, was transformed into a place of despair and anguish for the Roma.

In addition to the concentration camps, the Roma in Slovakia faced their own share of hardships. Forced labor camps became the grim reality for many Roma individuals, as they were compelled to toil under harsh conditions, contributing their sweat and labor to the German war effort. These labor camps, with their primitive living conditions and grueling work assignments, further tested the endurance and resilience of the Roma.

Amidst the darkness, it is noteworthy that Roma population in Slovakia experienced relatively better conditions compared to their counterparts in Bohemia and Moravia. Their involvement in labor camps, while undoubtedly challenging and arduous, offered a sliver of hope for survival in the midst of the war's brutality.

However, tragically, the Roma who remained in Bohemia and Moravia largely disappeared from the annals of history. Their voices were silenced, their stories untold. The descendants of the few survivors serve as poignant reminders of the irreplaceable loss suffered by the Moravian and Czech Roma communities during this harrowing period.

Out of the concentration camp prisoners, a mere 500 individuals managed to find their way back to their homes. This staggering statistic stands as a stark testament to the immense destruction and devastation inflicted upon the Roma people. It is important to recognize that the current Roma population in the Czech Republic, estimated to be between 250,000 to 300,000 individuals, primarily comprises waves of migration from Slovakia. This fact underscores the lasting impact of the war and its aftermath on the Roma population in Czechoslovakia, whose history continues to be shaped by the echoes of this dark chapter.

The Nazis and Romani People

During the dark and harrowing period of Nazi rule, the oppressive machinery of persecution and extermination extended its reach beyond the Jewish population to include other marginalized groups. Among these were the Roma and Sinti communities, deliberately targeted by the Nazis starting in 1943. The implementation of a ruthless plan mandated the transportation of individuals classified as "Gypsies and Gypsy half-breeds" from all territories under Nazi control to Auschwitz concentration camp, regardless of their social status, occupation, or property ownership. This systematic eradication, driven by notions of biological and racial superiority, dealt a devastating blow to a significant segment of the Roma population, which had already been undergoing assimilation processes.

In the aftermath of the war, surviving Roma individuals faced a daunting challenge: the concealment and erasure of their true ethnic origins from public consciousness. The need to protect themselves and future generations led many to suppress their Roma heritage, as its acknowledgment posed a potential threat to their safety and well-being. The original Czech and Moravian Roma community, which had existed prior to the war, experienced a profound decline, with their numbers reduced to a mere 1,000 individuals. This sobering reality confronted the Roma population in our country in the immediate post-war period.

The "Gypsy camp" at Auschwitz-Birkenau stands as a tragic and dark chapter in human history. Established in 1943 within the confines of Auschwitz II-Birkenau, this designated section of the concentration camp held 20,923 Roma individuals, each marked with a black triangle denoting them as "antisocial." Enduring deplorable living conditions, constant hunger, rampant disease, and systematic abuse, Roma people within the camp faced unspeakable horrors. Dr. Josef Mengele, infamously known as the "Angel of Death," subjected some Roma prisoners to horrific experiments, particularly targeting pregnant women and twins. Survival often relied on being transferred to other camps, as the conditions within the "Gypsy camp" remained unbearably grim.

In 1944, as the tides of war shifted, able-bodied Roma prisoners were dispatched deeper into German territory, leaving behind the elderly and mothers with children. It was on the night of August 2-3, 1944, that a grim and horrifying event unfolded. A total of 2,897 people, including hundreds of prisoners from the Czech lands, were forcefully herded into gas chambers, their lives mercilessly extinguished. Their bodies were disposed of in mass graves near the dormant crematorium, leaving behind a haunting testament to the depths of human cruelty.

The majority of Roma deported from the Protectorate of Bohemia and Moravia did not survive the horrors they endured. While exact numbers remain elusive, only 583 former Roma prisoners managed to return to the Czech lands after the war. This catastrophic loss marked the near-annihilation of the Czech Roma community, including those residing in Moravia. Tragically, the so-called "Gypsy camp" at Auschwitz-Birkenau claimed the lives of nearly 20,000 Roma and Sinti individuals from various countries, adding to the staggering toll of human suffering.

Estimates of Roma casualties during the Second World War vary between 250,000 and 500,000 individuals, a figure that casts a long and haunting shadow over the Roma community.

Roma Nationality

In the aftermath of World War II, the Roma population embarked on a transformative journey, experiencing significant societal, cultural, and value-based changes. Over the past four decades, and particularly in recent years, the Roma community, now officially recognized as a distinct nationality, has undergone shifts in its internal structure, population size, and geographic distribution. These transformations have resulted in a heightened sense of differentiation among various ethnic subgroups within the Roma community, leading to the emergence of a new social hierarchy.

The former socialist state of Czechoslovakia pursued efforts to assimilate and socially integrate the Roma population into the majority society. However, these endeavors proved flawed and unattainable. The focus was centered on "equalizing socio-economic and cultural backwardness," forming the foundation of what was termed the "solution to the Roma question." Yet, the reality has always been, and continues to be, an interethnic issue of coexistence between two distinct cultures. This coexistence is complicated by deep-rooted prejudices in the mutual relations between the Roma and the majority population, with recent years witnessing an alarming rise in racist sentiments against the Roma.

While improvements have been observed in the socio-economic status of many Roma individuals, evident in their standard of living, material culture, and educational opportunities, unintended consequences have emerged due to the disregard for the ethnic and cultural specificities of the Roma community. Over the span of four decades, the systematic suppression of traditional Roma values encompassing their way of life, culture, and language has led some Roma, particularly young families in urban areas, to feel a sense of shame regarding their Roma heritage. Consequently, they have ceased speaking the Romani language and failed to transmit it to future generations. In their pursuit of integration, they gradually severed their connection to their ethnic and national identity, as these identities and their unique characteristics were neither accepted nor acknowledged.

These transformations have not solely impacted social dynamics; they have also fundamentally reshaped the Romani way of life and cultural practices, producing both positive and negative consequences. On one hand, these changes have fostered increased inter-ethnic relationships and a stronger sense of identity preservation, particularly among Roma men. On the other hand, the traditional Roma community, with its established internal laws and norms, has experienced significant fragmentation. The previous codes and rigid value systems that governed group behavior have been disrupted, often without adequate replacement by more adaptable and effective norms.

Despite the challenges they have faced, the Roma have demonstrated resilience, adapting to their circumstances while preserving their unique identity and cultural practices. Today, the Romani community in the Czech Republic continues to uphold and celebrate its cultural heritage, passing down traditions, languages, and stories from one generation to the next. Additionally, they make significant contributions to various aspects of Czech society, including music, arts, literature, and activism, all while advocating for their rights and recognition.

The arrival of the Romani people in the Czech lands represents an essential chapter in the nation's history, shedding light on the complexities of migration, cultural diversity, and the ongoing quest for societal inclusivity and understanding. It invites us to delve into the enduring legacy of the Romani people and explore the evolving dynamics of a multicultural society.

Discrimination

Throughout the annals of history, the Romani people have confronted significant challenges and endured discrimination as a marginalized and nomadic group. Their distinct cultural identity, language, and nomadic lifestyle have rendered them susceptible to prejudice, stereotypes, and social exclusion within the societies they have encountered.

Discrimination against the Romani people, commonly known as Gypsy or Roma discrimination, has been pervasive across various countries and regions, including the Czech lands. The roots of this discrimination are multifaceted, intertwined with historical, social, economic, and cultural factors.

Deeply ingrained prejudice and enduring stereotypes have been key drivers of discrimination against the Romani people. Negative portrayals and misconceptions have perpetuated harmful stereotypes, associating Romani individuals with criminality, laziness, or untrustworthiness. These stereotypes have fueled discrimination in multiple spheres of life, including employment, education, housing, and access to healthcare.

The nomadic lifestyle historically embraced by the Romani people has also contributed to their marginalization. Nomadic communities often face obstacles in accessing essential services, adequate infrastructure, and recognition of their rights. Consequently, a cycle of poverty and social exclusion has arisen, further intensifying the discrimination endured by Romani individuals and communities.

Institutionalized discrimination against the Romani people is exemplified through discriminatory policies and practices. These encompass forced assimilation initiatives, such as removing Romani children from their families and placing them in state-run institutions, erasing their cultural heritage, and perpetuating a cycle of marginalization. Furthermore, the Romani people have encountered restrictions on their freedom of movement, housing segregation, and unequal treatment within the justice system.

The mistreatment and discrimination experienced by the Romani people have inflicted enduring and profound effects on their social and economic well-being. High poverty rates, limited access to quality education, and restricted employment opportunities are among the consequences of systemic discrimination. These perpetuate a cycle of disadvantage, impeding Romani individuals and communities in their quest to overcome the barriers they confront.

In recent times, endeavors have been undertaken to address these issues and foster greater social inclusion and equality for the Romani people. Advocacy groups, human rights organizations, and governments have united in combatting discrimination, raising awareness, and implementing policies that promote equal opportunities and accessible services for Romani individuals and communities.

However, achieving full equality and surmounting discrimination represent intricate and ongoing processes. They necessitate confronting deep-rooted prejudices, challenging stereotypes, fostering cultural understanding, and establishing inclusive societies that value diversity and respect the rights of all individuals, regardless of their ethnic background.

Lifestyle and Traditions

Across the vast expanse of time and space, the Romani people have woven a vibrant tapestry of traditions that forms an integral part of their profound cultural heritage. These enduring customs have served as pillars of resilience, identity, and communal cohesion for generations of Romani individuals and communities. In this chapter, we embark on a journey to explore the profound significance of Romani traditions and their transformative role in shaping the destiny of a resilient people.

Since time immemorial, the Romani have traversed diverse lands, guided by their cultural compass amidst ever-changing landscapes. Amidst the transient nature of their nomadic existence, these traditions have remained steadfast, providing a sense of continuity and belonging. They serve as a source of solace, anchoring the Romani to their roots and preserving their ancestral legacy.

As nomads, the Romani have assimilated and adapted the customs and practices of the regions they have encountered, weaving a rich tapestry of traditions that reflects the diversity of their encounters. Passed down through generations via oral tradition and lived experiences, these age-old customs form the very fabric of Romani identity. From the rhythmic melodies of their music and the captivating movements of their dances to the timeless wisdom embedded in their proverbs and folklore, each tradition serves as a testament to the collective memory of the Romani people.

Within the Romani community, traditions foster a profound sense of communal cohesion. They transcend geographical boundaries, forging a shared identity among dispersed individuals and families. Through their adherence to these cherished customs, Romani communities find solace and connection, forming a resilient network that endures even in the face of physical separation.

These traditions, rooted in spirituality and belief systems, serve as guiding beacons for the Romani people. Grounded in a reverence for nature, ancestral spirits, and a diverse array of religious influences, Romani traditions offer solace, protection, and spiritual guidance in the arduous journey of life. From sacred rituals to the veneration of ancestors, these practices establish a profound connection to a spiritual realm that transcends temporal and spatial boundaries.

Moreover, Romani traditions bear witness to the remarkable resilience of a people who have withstood centuries of discrimination and marginalization. They embody the stories of strength, survival, and unwavering determination that have propelled the Romani through the trials of history. Embedded within these traditions are the narratives of triumph over adversity, reminding us of the indomitable spirit that continues to propel the Romani forward.

By preserving and honoring these cherished traditions, the Romani ensure the perpetuation of their cultural heritage for future generations. Each celebration, dance, song, and proverb carry within it the wisdom and legacy of their ancestors, ensuring that their voices resonate through the corridors of time. Through the preservation of these customs, the Romani people forge a bridge between the past, the present, and the future, embracing their history while inspiring future generations to carry the torch of their remarkable journey.

In unraveling the significance of Romani traditions, we gain profound insights into the intricate tapestry of their culture, history, and enduring spirit. As we navigate the pages of their remarkable journey, we come to understand the indomitable strength and resilience that define the Romani people.

Days of the Wagons

The Romani people's reliance on wagons during the bygone era reflects a significant chapter in their history. These wagons, commonly known as vardos or caravans, were far more than mere modes of transportation. They embodied a profound sense of identity, freedom, and adventure that characterized the Romani way of life.

Imbued with remarkable craftsmanship, the wagons were meticulously designed to cater to the unique needs of the Romani people. Constructed on sturdy wooden frames with durable wheels suitable for diverse terrains and extensive journeys, these wagons showcased ingenious space utilization. Compartments were thoughtfully integrated, accommodating sleeping arrangements, storage areas, and functional living quarters.

The Romani people's skilled craftsmanship and deep-rooted cultural heritage found expression in the ornate adornments of their wagons. Elaborate carvings, vibrant colors, and decorative elements served as visual testaments to their artistic prowess and individuality. These wagons transcended mere utilitarian objects and became captivating works of art, evoking curiosity and fascination.

Functioning as mobile homes, the wagons provided the Romani families with a sense of shelter, comfort, and familiarity wherever their nomadic lifestyle led them. Within the wagons, one would find carefully arranged essentials such as beds, storage spaces for personal belongings, and compact cooking areas. Furthermore, their design facilitated easy disassembly and reassembly, allowing for seamless adaptation as they traversed different territories.

The Romani people's nomadic way of life was epitomized by their travel in caravans, forming close-knit communities on the road. These caravans enabled the preservation of their cultural traditions and facilitated social interaction, as temporary campsites, bender tents, or awnings were set up alongside the wagons. Such spaces served as hubs for communal activities, including cooking, storytelling, and forging social connections.

These wagons were not mere vehicles; they embodied ideals of independence, self-sufficiency, and resilience that were intrinsic to the Romani way of life. The wagons facilitated the Romani people's constant pursuit of new horizons, unexplored territories, and the preservation of their unique cultural identity.

While the Romani people have gradually embraced modern ways of life, the legacy of their wagon-dwelling ancestors endures in their cultural heritage, traditions, and the enduring symbolism of the wagon as a cherished relic of their collective history. These wagons serve as tangible reminders of a bygone era, evoking reflections on the Romani people's journey through time and the profound impact of their nomadic lifestyle on their collective identity.

Family and Hospitality

At the core of Romani traditions lies an unyielding reverence for the institution of family and the intricate web of kinship ties. Extended families reside in close proximity, forming a tightly knit network that permeates every aspect of Romani life.

One enduring aspect that characterizes Roma society is the profound significance attributed to family and kinship bonds. Families occupy a paramount position in the lives of Roma individuals, with the concept of extended family or kinship, commonly referred to as "fajta" or "famelija," assuming a central role.

Within these extended familial units, often referred to as "strong clans," certain members hold greater authority and wield influence over others. However, the solidarity and mutual support among family units remain robust, as individuals come together to provide assistance and aid. It is worth noting that even within contemporary Romani cultural and political spheres, influential figures and organizations often emerge from specific families interconnected by deep-seated kinship ties. Nonetheless, this familial association can occasionally give rise to rivalries and conflicts, leading to a lack of unity within the broader Romani socio-political movement.

Family occupies a sacred space within Romani culture. The bonds that tie individuals together extend beyond mere blood relations, encompassing a collective identity and a shared journey. Generations reside together, nurturing a profound sense of belonging and fostering a support system that weathers the storms of life. Whether in times of celebration or solace, family gatherings become sacred arenas where stories are shared, laughter resounds, and traditions are passed down from one generation to the next.

In earlier times, an unwritten code of "pure blood" governed many Roma groups, forbidding intermarriage with individuals from different ethnic backgrounds. However, the practice of endogamy, particularly prevalent among the Olaska Roma, has gradually waned in recent years. Today, such restrictions hold limited validity, not only among different Roma groups but also concerning unions with non-Roma partners. Consequently, inter-ethnic marriages, such as Roma-Czech, Roma-Slovak, and others, are on the rise, signaling significant shifts in the Roma community's values and social standing, particularly in urban areas of the Czech Republic and Moravia.

Hospitality reigns supreme within Romani households. Renowned for their warmth and friendliness, Romani people extend unwavering respect and generosity to their guests. Visitors are embraced as honored family members, welcomed with open arms and hearts. Shared meals transform into symphonies of flavors, uniting individuals from diverse backgrounds in a communal culinary experience that transcends language barriers.

Alongside the feast, storytelling takes center stage, interweaving history, folklore, and wisdom to create a tapestry of shared experiences that shapes the collective memory of the Romani community.

Romani hospitality encompasses more than a mere act of kindness; it is a sacred ritual that fosters connection and unity. Within the walls of a Romani home, strangers are transformed into friends, and cultural differences dissolve in the warmth of shared experiences. Through their open-heartedness, the Romani create spaces where individuals from all walks of life can find solace, acceptance, and a profound sense of belonging.

Family and hospitality have endured throughout the ages, providing a resilient foundation for the Romani people. Despite the adversities faced, including historical marginalization and discrimination, these pillars have sustained the Romani community, serving as anchors rooted in their identity, culture, and values. It is through these enduring aspects that the Romani navigate the complexities of the world with resilience and grace.

Religion and Spirituality

Religion and spirituality occupy an indelible place within the rich tapestry of Romani traditions, interweaving with every aspect of their existence. While there is no singular faith universally embraced by all Roma, diverse religious traditions and denominations find a home within different groups of the Roma community. Catholics, including Manouche, Mercheros, and Sinti; Muslims, such as Ashkali and Romanlar; Pentecostals, including Kalderash and Lovari; Protestants, represented by Travellers; Anglicans, observed by some; and Baptists, practiced by certain Roma individuals, are among the various religious affiliations found among the Roma. This religious diversity reflects the multilayered spiritual expressions and cultural influences that enrich the Roma community.

The Roma have embraced an inclusive and syncretic approach to religious beliefs, drawing from a mosaic of faiths that have shaped their spiritual landscape throughout history. Christianity, with its enduring influence, intertwines biblical teachings with unique interpretations forged by Romani perspectives. Islam, introduced through encounters with Muslim societies, strikes a deep resonance within specific groups, offering solace, guidance, and spiritual grounding.

Moreover, vestiges of ancient Hindu customs, echoing the ancestral origins of the Romani people in Northern India, continue to leave their imprint on spiritual practices and rituals. Additionally, indigenous spiritual traditions, deeply rooted in nature worship and animistic beliefs, infuse Romani spirituality with an intrinsic reverence for the natural world and the spirits of their ancestors.

Central to Romani religious and spiritual practices lies the notion of divine protection. Through their faith, Romani individuals seek solace, placing their trust in benevolent forces that safeguard and guide them through life's trials and tribulations. Prayers, rituals, and offerings are conducted to invoke divine intervention, ensuring the well-being of their families, communities, and journeys. Romani spirituality, intricately woven with the cycles of nature, celebrates the interconnectedness of all living beings, underscoring the profound reverence the Romani people hold for the earth, water, fire, and air.

Ancestral spirits occupy a significant place within Romani spirituality, serving as a bridge between the past and the present. Romani individuals honor and revere their ancestors, recognizing their wisdom, seeking their guidance, and relying on their protection. Rituals and ceremonies pay homage to these ancestral spirits, fostering a tangible connection that transcends the confines of time and space. Through these rituals, passed down through generations, the Romani people forge an unbroken bond with their rich ancestral heritage.

From the recitation of prayers to the observance of fasting periods, from the performance of traditional dances to the participation in communal worship, we delve into the intricate tapestry of beliefs and customs that constitute the bedrock of Romani spirituality. We also explore the roles of spiritual leaders within Romani communities, serving as mediators between the divine and the earthly realms, and their invaluable contributions to the preservation and transmission of spiritual knowledge.

Romani religion and spirituality extend beyond mere rituals and ceremonies, permeating every facet of life, from birth to death and all the moments in between. It serves as a wellspring of solace, guidance, and unity, resonating deeply within Romani communities and nurturing their collective strength, resilience, and unwavering connection to the sacred. This chapter sheds light on the profound spiritual journey of the Romani people, illuminating their enduring faith, deep-rooted traditions, and the eternal bond they share with the divine.

Festivals and Celebrations

Festivals and annual celebrations occupy a sacred space within Romani traditions, uniting communities to commemorate significant events. These joyous occasions showcase cultural practices adorned in traditional costumes, accompanied by the rhythmic cadence of music and the tantalizing flavors of culinary delights. Each festivity amplifies the diverse cultural heritage of the Romani people, encapsulating their vibrant collective spirit.

Romani culture is rich with vibrant festivals and celebrations that showcase the Romani people's beauty, traditions, and artistry. These events serve as important cultural milestones, bringing together Romani communities worldwide to honor their heritage, share their talents, and foster a sense of unity and pride.

One such notable festival is the Romani Festival, an international gathering held in various countries, including Spain, Romania, and the United Kingdom. This grand celebration spans several days and features a diverse program of concerts, performances, workshops, exhibitions, and film screenings. It provides a platform for Romani artists to showcase their talents and allows for cultural exchange and appreciation.

In the heart of Prague, Czech Republic, the Khamoro festival takes center stage. With its name meaning "Sun," Khamoro is one of the largest Romani festivals in Europe. It captivates audiences with a week-long extravaganza of music, dance, and cultural showcases. Romani artists and performers come together to demonstrate their skills, while workshops and exhibitions offer a deeper understanding of Romani culture and traditions.

In the Balkans, the Ederlezi festival holds great significance among Romani communities. Also known as "Herdeljezi" or "Đurđevdan," this lively celebration marks the arrival of spring. It is characterized by spirited music, traditional dancing, feasting, and the lighting of bonfires. Ederlezi honors Saint George and symbolizes renewal, fertility, and the triumph of life over darkness.

Flamenco, a genre deeply connected to Romani culture, finds its moment in the Flamenco Biennial in Seville, Spain. This renowned event celebrates the artistry of flamenco, showcasing performances, music, dance, and workshops. While not exclusive to the Romani community, the festival offers an immersive experience of the passionate world of flamenco, influenced by the rich Romani heritage.

April 8th holds special significance as Roma Day or International Roma Day, commemorating the historic First World Romani Congress in London in 1971. This day is a global celebration of Romani culture and a platform to raise awareness about Romani rights and issues. Across the world, various events, discussions, and cultural activities are organized to honor the contributions and resilience of the Romani people.

In Russia, the Festival of Gypsy Culture in Moscow shines a spotlight on the traditions, music, dance, and craftsmanship of the

Romani community. This festival serves as a platform for Romani artists, performers, and artisans to showcase their talents and share their cultural heritage. Exhibitions, concerts, workshops, and interactive events engage the wider society, fostering understanding and appreciation of Romani culture.

These Romani festivals and celebrations are not only joyful occasions but also significant cultural milestones that preserve and celebrate the rich heritage of the Romani people. They provide a space for artistic expression, cultural exchange, and community cohesion, allowing the Romani community to thrive and the wider society to appreciate the unique contributions of this vibrant culture.

Romani Weddings

Romani weddings have perpetually fascinated the human imagination, invoking a sense of adventure and mystique. From the intricate pre-wedding rituals to the enduring post-wedding customs, these distinctive practices infuse an ethereal quality into every ceremony, crafting memories that endure for a lifetime.

Within the confines of this section, we embark on a comprehensive exploration of Gypsy wedding traditions, delving into the minutiae of attire, ceremonies, receptions, decorations, and symbols that are exclusive to this vibrant and culturally rich tradition.

At the very core of Romani weddings lies a vibrant mosaic of colors, distinctive customs, and captivating attire. From the radiant bride and groom to the esteemed guests, each individual adorns themselves in traditional Romani garments that encapsulate their cultural heritage and personal style. These elaborate and meticulously crafted garments are not merely decorative but hold profound symbolic significance, reflecting the values, beliefs, and social identities of the Romani community.

The Bride and Groom

The bride assumes a central role in the Romani wedding, emanating beauty and grace as she glides in a flowing skirt that cascades with every step. These skirts, meticulously crafted from sumptuous fabrics such as silk or velvet, bear witness to the artistry and craftsmanship of Romani traditions. Intricate embroidery adorns the fabric, intricately weaving a narrative that reflects the rich cultural heritage and skilled hands that brought it to life. Elaborate dresses, embellished with ruffles, lace, or sequins, amplify the opulence and femininity that permeate the occasion.

Completing her regal ensemble, the bride dons an ornate headdress that emanates an aura of majesty. With meticulous placement, coins and jewelry come together in a harmonious symphony, creating a dazzling display atop her head. Heavy gold necklaces, cascading earrings, bracelets, anklets, and rings are thoughtfully chosen to enhance her radiance and symbolize her elevated status on this special day.

Meanwhile, the groom exudes strength and elegance through his attire. A foundation of a white shirt with intricately embroidered sleeves is accentuated by black trousers or jeans tucked into sturdy boots. However, it is the exquisitely adorned waistcoat that truly elevates his look. It showcases a tapestry of intricate patterns and designs, serving as a testament to the craftsmanship of Romani artisans. A vibrant sash, cinched around his waist, adds a splash of color and flair. Crowned with a wide-brimmed hat adorned with feathers or ribbons, the groom exudes an aura of charisma and confidence, embodying the significance of the occasion.

Not to be overshadowed, the guests attending a Romani wedding actively participate in the sartorial spectacle. Women grace the celebration in flowing skirts adorned with vibrant hues, harmoniously paired with brightly colored tops that reflect their individual style. Men, too, pay homage to tradition, donning shirts intricately embellished with designs that capture the eye. Trousers, carefully tucked into boots, complete their ensemble. Some guests may choose to express their unique identity by adding scarves or hats as accessories, celebrating the vivacity and cultural richness of the Romani community.

Within the realm of Romani weddings, attire transcends its mere physicality, assuming the profound role of a symbol of cultural heritage and a joyous proclamation of identity. Adorned with a symphony of vibrant hues, opulent textiles, and intricate motifs, the Romani community weaves together a visual feast that captivates onlookers. Through this extraordinary display, they invite others to partake in the beauty and significance of this remarkable celebration, fostering an appreciation for the cultural tapestry that envelops the Romani wedding experience.

Sacred Union

Romani wedding ceremonies are woven with threads of tradition that carry profound symbolism and cultural significance. These rituals, passed down through generations, serve as a testament to the enduring love shared by the couple and solidify the sacred bond that unites them.

At the core of the ceremony lies the exchange of vows, a moment that transcends time and space, marking a profound commitment between the betrothed. Standing before their loved ones, Romani couples pledge their love and fidelity, promising to navigate life's journey hand in hand. Whether they recite traditional vows that have withstood the test of time or craft heartfelt words of their own, the couple's promises resonate with the depth of their devotion and the power of their union.

Rings play a pivotal role in these wedding ceremonies, carrying profound symbolism. Before finding their place on the couple's fingers, the rings undergo a special blessing. Both families come together, offering their collective love and support as they bless the rings. This act signifies the eternal love and dedication shared between the couple, while also serving as a unifying force that brings the families together in celebration and support of the couple's union.

Another cherished tradition is the lighting of the unity candle. Two separate flames, representing the individual lives and journeys of the couple, merge into a single flame. As the couple ignites the candle's wick, their lives blend harmoniously, symbolizing their unity in marriage while honoring their unique identities within the union. The warm glow of the candle radiates hope and love, guiding the couple on their shared path. During this poignant moment, family members and close friends offer heartfelt wishes and blessings, ensuring that the couple's married life is filled with joy, prosperity, and everlasting happiness.

The Reception Party

Romani wedding receptions are a vibrant celebration that embodies various cherished traditions and customs. The air resonates with the enchanting melodies of traditional instruments like violins and accordions, creating an irresistible energy that sets the stage for lively dancing and revelry. The culinary delights take center stage, featuring a delectable array of dishes such as stuffed cabbage rolls and potato pancakes, prepared with meticulous care and imbued with the love and culinary heritage passed down through generations.

Gift-giving holds a significant place in Romani wedding receptions, as guests offer tokens of well-wishes and blessings to the newlywed couple. These gifts encompass a range of items, including monetary contributions, jewelry symbolizing eternal love and prosperity, and practical items that represent security and a flourishing future. Each gift carries the hopes and aspirations of the giver, contributing to the collective joy and celebration of the occasion.

The reception venue itself is adorned with enchanting decorations and symbols that hold profound meaning and cultural significance. The color palette weaves together vibrant hues of red, yellow, orange, green, blue, and purple, evoking a sense of joy and celebration.

Flowers, such as roses, lilies, daisies, and carnations, grace the surroundings with delicate beauty and intoxicating scents. Thoughtfully chosen floral arrangements, including bouquets and centerpieces, are carefully selected to symbolize love, joy, and purity.

Romani wedding receptions pay homage to the cherished traditions passed down through generations within the Roma Gypsy community. The groom presents the bride with a bouquet of flowers, an act of respect and a symbolic request for her hand in marriage. The exchange of rings and coins during the ceremony signifies the couple's eternal love and commitment.

Following the ceremony, the newlyweds embark on a horse and cart ride, symbolizing their union, accompanied by loved ones. A ceremonial meal is shared, bringing together families and friends to partake in the festivities. Traditional dances performed by the bride and groom add an elegant touch to the celebration, culminating in a joyous feast enjoyed by all.

A Romani wedding reception infuses the celebration with vibrant music, lively dancing, tantalizing cuisine, and heartfelt traditions. It serves as a time for families, friends, and the wider community to come together, sharing in the joy and unity of the newlywed couple as they embark on their journey of love and togetherness.

Music

Music is paramount in Romani culture, serving as a profound medium of expression, storytelling, and cultural identity. Rooted in centuries of tradition and enriched by diverse influences, Romani music carries a deep sense of history, emotion, and celebration.

The essence of traditional Romani music lies in its vibrant melodies, intricate rhythms, and captivating performances. Romani singers, renowned for their passionate and soulful delivery, bring forth the distinct vocal style that characterizes this music. The lyrics of Romani songs encapsulate the experiences, joys, and struggles of the Romani people, reflecting themes of love, longing, freedom, and cultural pride.

Instrumentation plays a vital role in Romani music, as various traditional instruments contribute to its unique sound. The guitar, accordion, violin, cimbalom, and tambourine are commonly used instruments, each bringing its own timbre and adding depth and richness to the overall musical experience.

The infectious rhythms and energetic performances of Romani music have left an indelible mark on the world of music. Romani musicians have significantly shaped and influenced various genres, including jazz, flamenco, and Balkan music. In addition, their improvisational skills, virtuosity, and deep connection to the music have garnered international recognition and admiration.

Romani music festivals and gatherings serve as vital spaces for musicians and audiences to come together, celebrating their culture and sharing the joy of music. These events showcase the diversity within Romani music, featuring different regional styles, dance forms, and vocal traditions. The lively atmosphere, filled with dancing, clapping, and singing, creates an immersive experience that transcends language barriers and unites people in the universal language of music.

During the nineteenth century, urban Gypsy choral groups significantly shaped a distinctive musical style known as "Gypsy Romance." This style emerged as a fusion of Russian folk and urban love songs, influenced by the melodic embellishments and expressive techniques found in Romani singing. Singers, often female, deliver these heartfelt compositions with a characteristic vibrato and semitone decoration, accompanied by the melodic strains of violins and guitars. While Russians cherish this style for its melodramatic and romantic qualities, it should be noted that various other styles of Romani music are lesser-known yet equally captivating in their own right. These diverse musical traditions showcase the Romani people's rich cultural heritage and artistic prowess, adding depth and intrigue to the vibrant tapestry of world music. Beyond its artistic value, Romani music serves as a crucial link to the Romani people's cultural heritage and collective memory. It is a means of preserving and passing down traditions, stories, and values from generation to generation. Through music, Romani communities maintain their cultural identity, foster resilience, and assert their rightful place in the tapestry of human history.

Romani music is an integral part of Romani culture, capturing the essence of their experiences and aspirations. Its spirited melodies, soulful vocals, and rhythmic vitality have touched hearts, bridged cultures, and inspired countless musicians worldwide. By embracing and celebrating their musical heritage, Romani people continue to contribute to the rich tapestry of global music, reminding us of the power of music to transcend boundaries and connect us all.

Dance

In the intricate tapestry of Romani culture, dance weaves a mesmerizing narrative, an embodiment of the Romani spirit, and a vibrant expression of their rich heritage. Within each movement lies a profound significance, a testament to joy, celebration, and the unbreakable bonds of community. Romani dance captivates all who partake in its rhythmic embrace, vividly portraying resilience and cultural identity transcending time and borders.

Among the diverse Romani dance styles, one stands out as a shining symbol of Romani culture: flamenco. Originating in Spain, flamenco intertwines with the Romani narrative, its dynamic movements and expressive gestures echoing the depths of the Romani experience. With percussive footwork, graceful arm movements, and intricate hand gestures, flamenco becomes a language of its own, a conduit for stories and emotions that dance through the souls of those who perform it.

Romani dance extends far beyond the realms of flamenco, encompassing a kaleidoscope of styles rooted in various regions. Traditional Romani circles and folk dances from the Balkans to Eastern Europe add to the tapestry of movement. These dances captivate with their intricate formations, synchronized movements, and energetic footwork, painting a mesmerizing tableau of cultural expression.

Yet, Romani dance is not confined to the stage it thrives in the beating heart of community gatherings, where weddings, festivals, and social occasions become vibrant stages for Romani dancers to unite, share their skills, and strengthen their bonds. These joyous events are infused with lively music, adorned with vibrant costumes, and animated by the exuberant performances of Romani dancers, creating an atmosphere of pure jubilation and unity.

The transmission of Romani dance traditions is a cherished intergenerational practice rooted in the passing down knowledge and skills from elders to the younger generations. Romani communities preserve dance forms through this sacred connection, safeguarding their cultural legacy with pride, identity, and a sense of continuity. The power of dance lies in its artistic expression and its role as a vessel for heritage, connecting generations and forging an unbreakable chain of cultural identity.

Romani dance's influence extends far beyond its community, resonating within the hearts of artists and enthusiasts worldwide. Its rhythmic patterns, expressive movements, and infectious energy have ignited the imaginations of choreographers and inspired the evolution of dance forms across the globe. With its timeless spirit, Romani dance continues to shape the fabric of the world's dance heritage, leaving an indelible mark on the stage and in the hearts of those who bear witness.

Through the language of dance, Romani individuals assert their cultural heritage, reclaim their narratives, and defy stereotypes. It becomes a vessel of cultural resistance and a medium for self-expression, allowing Romani dancers to celebrate their identity, assert their presence, and share their unique stories with the world. While the origins of Romani dance may fade into the mists of time, its enduring presence and profound significance in the Romani cultural tapestry remain an undeniable testament to the resilience and beauty of a people whose vibrant spirit dances on.

Circus

In the annals of history, the bond between circuses and the Roma people reveals a captivating tale that transcends mere coincidence. At the heart of this extraordinary connection lies the nomadic lifestyle that defined the Roma community. Their endless journey, marked by constant movement and adaptability, found a remarkable parallel in the circus world. Within its vibrant domain, the Roma discovered a means of livelihood and a sanctuary where their unique talents and cultural heritage could flourish.

As the Roma traversed vast landscapes, traversing towns and villages every fortnight, their fate seemed destined to intertwine with the allure of the circus. This realm of captivating spectacles and enchanting performances beckoned to the Roma, offering them an ideal occupation. The transient nature of circus life provided the perfect canvas for their itinerant existence, where they could seamlessly blend their artistic prowess with the allure of the Big Top.

In the colorful tapestry of the circus, the Roma found a harmonious convergence of their innate abilities and the demands of this enchanting world. Their captivating music, mesmerizing dance, and awe-inspiring acrobatics transformed them into invaluable contributors to the grand spectacle. In addition, the Roma established a sense of identity and purpose through their participation, celebrating their cultural heritage on stages adorned with splendor and wonder.

Amidst a society marred by discrimination and exclusion, the circus became an oasis of acceptance for the Roma. Within the vibrant circus community, they encountered a fellowship that transcended societal boundaries. The shared pursuit of artistry and the collective spirit of performance forged unbreakable bonds, offering solace and support to a people whose place in the wider world remained precarious.

Yet, while the circus served as a sanctuary for the Roma, it was not immune to the pervasive prejudice that plagued society. Stereotypes and exoticization persisted, casting a distorted lens upon the Roma's rich and diverse culture. However, with unwavering resilience, the Roma defied these misconceptions, leaving an indelible mark on the history of the circus.

Theater

Throughout history, the Roma community has woven threads of artistic brilliance that continue to mesmerize audiences. Beyond their renowned musical prowess, the Roma people have showcased remarkable acting abilities that have left indelible marks on the world of theater and performance. Throughout the ages, Roma actors traversed the landscapes, their talents taking center stage in itinerant theater companies and puppet theaters that roamed from village to village, captivating hearts and minds wherever they went. These skilled performers even established synthetic theaters, where spoken word seamlessly intertwined with music and dance, creating a magical fusion of storytelling and artistry.

As the Roma artists took to the streets, their performances ignited the imaginations of onlookers. With graceful dance routines and enchanting musical compositions, they created a sensory spectacle that transported audiences to realms of wonder and delight. Adding an extra layer of fascination to their street shows, Roma performers sometimes incorporated animals into their acts. Acrobatics became an extraordinary display of physical prowess, and the art of training animals, including bears and monkeys, became a captivating feat that further elevated their performances.

Within the Roma community, tales of talented individuals echoed through the ages as renowned theatrical families nurtured extraordinary skills that mesmerized audiences. Among them stood Matěj Kopecký, a founding figure of Czech puppetry whose name became synonymous with innovation and creativity. The famous acrobatic Berousky family dazzled spectators with their fearless displays of agility and strength, leaving crowds in awe of their daring feats.

As the 20th century unfolded, Romani families in Czechoslovakia embarked on an extraordinary venture, establishing their own smaller circuses that showcased their artistic prowess. These vibrant enclaves became sanctuaries where Romani artists and animal handlers could freely express their talents and share their unique heritage. Across distant lands, Romani artists continued to enrich the magical world of circuses, weaving their artistry into the very fabric of the spectacle.

Romani creativity thrives within dedicated theaters that serve as platforms for artistic expression. Noteworthy among these is the Macedonian Pralipe Theater, which found its footing in Germany under the visionary leadership of director Rahim Burhan. Born in Skopje, former Yugoslavia, this theater group rapidly garnered acclaim as they embarked on successful tours, leaving a trail of awards in their wake. Pralipe Theater stood as a beacon of cultural pride for the Roma community in Macedonia, a testament to the resilience and artistic spirit that resonated within their hearts.

Yet, the path of the Roma artists was not without its challenges. Political opposition cast shadows upon their endeavors, threatening to snuff out the vibrant flames of creativity. Financial and cultural hurdles loomed, posing formidable obstacles to the very existence of these artistic havens. In a twist of fate, salvation arrived through connections forged with the German Theater an der Ruhr in Mülheim. United under the shared vision of artistic director Dr. Robert Ciulli and dramaturg Dr. Helmut Schäfer, the Pralipe Theater found a new home, preserving its legacy and continuing its artistic journey on foreign soil.

In a remarkable convergence of cultures, the Roma Theater Pralipe graced the city of Prague in May 2001. As part of the esteemed Khamoro festival, their mesmerizing multimedia project, "Z 2001 - Ink under my skin," unfolded before captivated audiences. Through evocative storytelling and the power of their performances, the Roma Theater Pralipe revealed a world where creativity transcended barriers and ignited the collective spirit of those fortunate enough to witness their artistic tapestry.

In the vast cultural panorama of Slovakia, a luminous beacon of artistic brilliance emerges, illuminating the spirit and resilience of the

Roma community — the Romathan Theater. Since its inception in 1992, this theater has emerged as a powerful testament to the transformative power of art in Košice, providing a sanctuary where the Roma people find solace and a platform for self-expression. The very name of the theater, Romathan, resonates with profound significance, embodying a sacred space dedicated to the Roma, where their stories are woven with pride and fiery passion.

At the core of the captivating repertoire showcased by the Romathan Theater lies a rich tapestry of artistic endeavors. Roma folk art takes center stage, infusing their performances with a vibrant thread that connects them to their cultural heritage. The theater showcases plays written by Romani authors, their narratives steeped in the depths of their ancestral traditions, unfolding on the hallowed boards with an undeniable authenticity. Furthermore, the theater reimagines world classics through the lens of Roma artistry and sensibilities, breathing new life into these timeless works with a distinctive flair.

Music, a universal language that transcends borders, occupies a central role in the productions of the Romathan Theater. The evocative compositions of Roma composers grace the stage, resonating with soul-stirring melodies that have been nurtured and passed down through generations. Leading this artistic symphony is the eminent figure of Karel Adam, a luminary within the Roma community and a maestro in his own right. With his virtuoso skills on the violin and profound musical insight, Karel Adam breathes life into the theater's musical landscape, guiding the Orchestra of Folk Instruments with grace and unwavering passion.

The influence of the Romathan Theater extends far beyond the borders of Slovakia, captivating audiences across the globe. From the enchanting stages of England to the revered theaters of the Czech Republic, from the bustling cultural hubs of Hungary to the vibrant landscapes of Germany, Poland, Russia, and France, the Roma artistry radiates its brilliance, leaving an indelible mark on every stage it graces.

The exceptional contributions of the theater have garnered well-deserved recognition, including a coveted gold medal from Moscow and the honor of acknowledgment from the

President of the Slovak Republic, solidifying its position as a beacon of Roma cultural expression and artistic excellence.

Language

The Romani traditions are intrinsically intertwined with language, serving as a vital pillar of their cultural fabric. The Romani language, with its diverse array of dialects, not only fosters a sense of pride and identity but also functions as a powerful means of communication, cultural preservation, and resistance against assimilation. The ongoing endeavors to revitalize and safeguard the Romani language underscore its indispensable role in upholding and transmitting their rich cultural heritage.

Revisiting prevailing assumptions, linguists have put forth a compelling argument challenging the notion of multiple waves of migration by the ancestors of the Roma. Instead, a new perspective emerges, suggesting that the Roma embarked on a single, albeit extensive and possibly gradual, migration from India. This revision finds support in the shared language carried by the Roma upon their arrival in Europe during the 11th and 12th centuries. Subsequently, the diversification of Romani dialects occurred as a result of interactions with European languages, further shaping the linguistic landscape.

While Romani groups traversed medieval and early modern Europe independently, evidence indicates that they maintained connections and exchanges with one another. Notably, the appearance of similar original documents, known as "gleits," among various Romani groups serves as a testament to their ongoing contact and interaction. However, as time progressed, these intergroup connections gradually diminished, giving rise to greater regional differentiation within the Romani community.

Through a nuanced exploration of linguistic research and historical evidence, a more comprehensive understanding of the Roma people and the intricate web of their interconnectedness begins to unfold. While regional variations in experiences and customs may be evident, the Roma's shared heritage and aspirations for solidarity continue to shape their collective identity in the modern world, illuminating the resilience and dynamism of this remarkable ethnic group.

Dialects

The Romani language, encompassing a wide range of dialects, mirrors the diverse and dispersed nature of the Romani communities across the globe. Geographical separation, interactions with diverse cultures, and the assimilation of local languages have played pivotal roles in the evolution of these dialects. Exploring the intricate tapestry of Romani linguistic diversity, we encounter a mosaic of dialects, each with its own distinct features and regional nuances. Some notable examples include:

Vlax Romani

This is one of the most widespread dialects of Romani and is spoken by Romani communities in Eastern Europe, including the Czech Republic. It has several sub-dialects, such as Kalderash, Lovari, and Machvano.

Sinti Romani

This dialect is spoken by the Sinti people, who have historical roots in Central Europe. It is prevalent in countries like Germany, Austria, and the Czech Republic.

Carpathian Romani

This dialect is spoken by Romani communities in the Carpathian Mountains region, which includes parts of Slovakia, Ukraine, and Poland. It has its own distinct features and vocabulary.

Balkan Romani

This dialect is spoken by Romani communities in the Balkan region, including countries such as Serbia, Romania, Bulgaria, and Macedonia. It has various sub-dialects influenced by the local languages of these regions.

Iberian Romani

This dialect is spoken by Romani communities in Spain and Portugal. It has its unique characteristics and shows influences from the Spanish and Portuguese languages.

Scandinavian Romani

This dialect is spoken by Romani communities in Scandinavia, particularly in Sweden and Norway. It has developed its features influenced by the local languages of the region.

These are just a few examples of the diverse Romani dialects that exist. Each dialect has its distinct vocabulary, grammar, and pronunciation, reflecting Romani communities' historical migrations and interactions across different regions.

Romani Oral Tradition

Embedded within the fabric of Romani culture lies a profound appreciation for the power of oral tradition. Across generations, the transmission of historical accounts, moral teachings, and cultural wisdom takes place through the art of storytelling, proverbs, and folk tales. These narratives serve as vehicles of education, entertainment, and the preservation of cherished values, allowing Romani communities to maintain a strong connection to their past while navigating the complexities of the present.

The vibrant tapestry of Romani traditions weaves together a multitude of practices, celebrations, and values, illuminating the profound richness and diversity of their cultural heritage. These traditions, deeply rooted in historical experiences and shared memories, serve as pillars of resilience, identity, and communal cohesion for Romani individuals and communities. By nurturing and upholding these time-honored customs, the Romani people ensure the preservation of their cultural tapestry and the perpetuation of their collective memory, safeguarding their legacy for generations yet to come.

The significance of oral tradition within Romani culture cannot be overstated. It stands as a testament to the enduring power of storytelling, proverbs, and folk tales in preserving the collective memory, historical narratives, moral teachings, and cultural wisdom of the Romani people. Through these forms of expression, Romani heritage continues to thrive, providing a source of inspiration, guidance, and connection that transcends time and space.

Storytelling

Storytelling is a cherished tradition within Romani communities, with skilled storytellers captivating audiences of all ages with their tales. These stories carry many themes, including legendary heroes, moral dilemmas, love and romance, encounters with supernatural beings, and the struggles and triumphs of the Romani people throughout history. Through these narratives, the experiences and perspectives of the community are shared and passed on, fostering a sense of identity, resilience, and unity.

Proverbs

Proverbs, or wise sayings, play a significant role in Romani oral tradition. They encapsulate the collective wisdom, observations, and insights of the community. Proverbs are concise, memorable expressions that convey moral teachings, cultural norms, and practical advice. They provide guidance, provoke thought, and serve as valuable tools for teaching and instilling cultural values in younger generations.

Folk Tales

Folk tales are another important aspect of Romani oral tradition. These traditional stories are woven with elements of fantasy, magic, and everyday life, offering valuable insights into the Romani people's cultural beliefs, social customs, and historical experiences. In addition, folk tales often carry moral lessons, offering guidance on topics such as honesty, respect, loyalty, and the consequences of one's actions.

Through Within the tapestry of Romani culture, storytelling, proverbs, and folk tales emerge as vital conduits that transcend mere entertainment, assuming a profound educational and cultural role. Oral tradition becomes a repository of history, traditions, and values that might otherwise elude written records. Its intangible nature imparts a distinctive channel for transmitting cultural identity, fostering an unwavering sense of belonging and connection to Romani roots.

Moreover, oral tradition in Romani culture serves as a catalyst for communal participation and interaction. The storytelling sessions and gatherings are not passive engagements but active dialogues, inviting the audience to respond, question, and contribute to the unfolding narrative. This interactive dimension of oral tradition weaves a tapestry of community bonds, fostering dialogue and nurturing a shared experience that fortifies the collective sense of identity and cultural continuity.

In a world where written documentation may be scarce or inaccessible, oral tradition assumes the role of a living archive, carrying the weight of the Romani people's history, knowledge, and values. It stands as a custodian, ensuring that the experiences, struggles, and triumphs of past generations find a voice and resonate through time. Through the preservation and promotion of oral tradition, the cultural heritage of the Romani community remains vibrant and resilient, defying the eroding forces of forgetfulness.

By honoring and nurturing oral tradition, the Romani community embraces a profound responsibility, preserving their distinct identity, transmitting their cultural legacy, and celebrating the profound richness of their heritage. It is through this unwavering commitment that the Romani people safeguard and perpetuate their ancestral wisdom, offering future generations a wellspring of strength, knowledge, and inspiration embedded within the timeless narratives and cultural treasures interwoven into the very fabric of their oral tradition.

Historical Accounts

The Story of the Romani Migration

Passed down through generations, these narrative recounts the journey of the Romani people from their origins in northern India to their subsequent migration and settlement in various parts of the world. It provides insights into the historical experiences, challenges, and adaptations of the Romani community as they navigated different lands and encountered diverse cultures. Below is a sample of such a story.

Once upon a time, in a land far away, nestled amidst the majestic mountains and sprawling deserts of northern India, there lived a vibrant community known as the Romani people. Our ancestors roamed these lands for generations, cherishing our culture, language, and ancient traditions. But a time came when the winds of destiny whispered in our ears, urging us to embark on a remarkable journey.

With hearts full of longing and spirits ablaze with wanderlust, we left our beloved homeland, bidding farewell to the familiar sights and sounds that had woven the tapestry of our lives. Our wagons rolled across dusty roads, our horses carried us through valleys and over rivers, as we ventured forth into the great unknown.

Our migration took us far and wide, spanning continents and crossing vast oceans. We traversed ancient lands, encountering diverse peoples, and embracing the beauty of their cultures. Each step brought us closer to the realization that our Romani identity was both resilient and adaptable, capable of weaving itself into the fabric of new lands while retaining the essence of who we are.

In far-off lands, we faced challenges and hardships. The road was not always smooth, and our nomadic lifestyle often stirred the fears and prejudices of those we encountered. But with each trial, we drew strength from our shared history, our deep-rooted traditions, and the bonds that held us together as a community.

As we settled in new lands, we brought with us the melodies of our songs, the rhythms of our dances, and the stories etched into our hearts. We shared the beauty of our crafts, adorned with intricate patterns and vibrant colors that spoke of our ancestral heritage. Our language, the Romani tongue, echoed through bustling marketplaces and quiet campfires, connecting us to our past and shaping our future.

Through our migration, we became storytellers, weaving tales of resilience, love, and the enduring spirit of the Romani people. Our stories spoke of the trials we faced, the friendships we forged, and the bonds of family that held us tight. They carried the wisdom of our ancestors and the dreams of our children, reminding us of our shared journey and the strength that lies within us all.

Today, we honor our Romani heritage, celebrating the footsteps of our forebears and the legacy they left behind. We keep the flames of our traditions burning bright, passing down our stories from generation to generation, ensuring that the spirit of our migration lives on in the hearts and minds of our Romani brothers and sisters.

So gather around, my friends, as I share with you the tale of the Romani migration. Let us remember our roots, embrace our unique culture, and cherish the bonds that connect us all. For in our story, we find the power to unite, inspire, and keep our Romani flame burning bright.

The Resistance and Survival Stories

These narratives recount the struggles and resistance of the Romani people during times of oppression, discrimination, and persecution. They preserve accounts of resilience, acts of bravery, and the determination to preserve Romani identity and culture in the face of adversity. These stories offer historical insights into the challenges faced by the community and the resilience demonstrated by Romani individuals and communities. Below is a sample of such a story.

Once upon a time, in the depths of history, the Romani people faced a storm of oppression, discrimination, and persecution. But within the shadows, there flickered stories of resistance and survival, tales of bravery and defiance that echo through the ages.

Listen closely, my friends, as I share with you the stories of our people's strength and resilience. In the darkest of times, when hatred and cruelty reigned, the Romani community stood tall, their spirits unbroken.

During the time of the Nazis, our people faced unimaginable horrors. But in the face of such darkness, pockets of light emerged. Romani men, women, and children, heroes among us, displayed remarkable courage. They formed secret networks, offering protection and aid to their fellow brothers and sisters. Through whispers in the night, they shared vital information, nourishment for the hungry, and acts of defiance against the oppressors.

Bound by a shared struggle, the Romani people forged alliances with other persecuted communities. United, we stood against tyranny, transcending barriers of language and culture. In those moments of solidarity, the strength of our ancestors shone brightly, a testament to the power of unity.

But let us not forget, my friends, that our resistance did not end with that dark chapter. Throughout history, our community has faced discrimination and persecution, but we have not been silenced. Romani individuals, proud and strong, refused to let our voices be silenced. Artists, writers, and activists emerged, wielding the power of their words and talents to challenge stereotypes and fight for justice.

These stories, passed down through generations, speak of our unwavering spirit, our love for our heritage, and our determination to preserve our culture against all odds. They remind us that we are not defined solely by our suffering, but by our resilience and the power of our collective will.

Today, we gather around the fire, my friends, to honor the resistance and survival stories of our people. We remember those who came before us, who stood tall and faced adversity with unwavering courage. Their stories inspire us to stand against injustice, to celebrate our diversity, and to weave a future where all voices are heard and respected.

As we share these stories, let us carry them in our hearts, passing them down to our children and grandchildren. May these tales of resistance and survival continue to guide us, reminding us of the indomitable strength that lies within us, and the power of unity in the face of adversity.

Heroes and Heroines

Celebrated and notable figures within Romani history who have made significant contributions to their communities or have achieved legendary status. They honor individuals who have stood up for justice, fought against oppression, or demonstrated exceptional skills, talents, or leadership. These stories serve as a source of inspiration and cultural pride, preserving the memory and achievements of Romani heroes throughout history. Below is a sample of such a story.

Gather around, my dear listeners, as I share with you the tales of our Romani heroes and heroines, those extraordinary individuals who have left an indelible mark on our history. These are the legends and legends-in-the-making, celebrated figures who have risen above adversity, fought for justice, and led our people with strength and courage.

One such hero is Matéo Maximoff, a prolific Romani writer and historian who dedicated his life to preserving and sharing the stories and culture of our people. Through his writings, he shed light on the rich history, traditions, and struggles of the Romani community, ensuring that our heritage would not be forgotten. His works continue to inspire generations, instilling a sense of pride and unity among Romani individuals worldwide.

Another remarkable figure is Ceija Stojka, an Austrian-Romani artist, writer, and survivor of the Holocaust. Ceija courageously shared her personal experiences of the horrors endured during the Nazi regime, painting vivid images that depicted the resilience and strength of our people. Her artwork serves as a powerful testament to the Romani Holocaust, educating the world about our community's suffering and inspiring us to never forget.

In the realm of music, Django Reinhardt stands as a legend among legends. Born into a Sinti Romani family, Django defied societal expectations and became one of the greatest jazz guitarists of all time. His innovative style and virtuoso performances continue to captivate audiences, transcending boundaries and showcasing the immense talent and creativity of the Romani people.

Let us also remember our heroines, those remarkable women who have left an indelible impact on our community. One such heroine is

Rosa Taikon, a Swedish-Romani activist and advocate for Romani rights. Rosa fearlessly fought against discrimination, working tirelessly to challenge stereotypes and improve the lives of Romani individuals. Her dedication and determination continue to inspire us to this day, reminding us of the importance of raising our voices and standing up for justice.

These are just a few examples of the heroes and heroines who have graced our history. But let us not forget that each and every one of you, my dear listeners, has the potential to be a hero in your own right. Through acts of kindness, resilience, and courage, you contribute to the ongoing legacy of our people, leaving footprints for future generations to follow.

As we share these stories of our heroes and heroines, let us honor their memory and carry their legacy forward. May their bravery and accomplishments inspire us to continue striving for equality, justice, and the celebration of our Romani heritage. For in these stories, we find strength, pride, and a reminder that the power to make a difference lies within each and every one of us.

Moral Teachings

The Tale of Honesty and Integrity

This moral tale emphasizes the importance of honesty, integrity, and the consequences of dishonesty. It may revolve around a central character who faces a moral dilemma and must make choices that align with their values. The story conveys moral lessons, teaching the significance of truthfulness, accountability, and the impact of one's actions on others. Below is a sample of such a story.

Once upon a time, in a Romani village nestled amidst the rolling hills, there lived a young man named Emil. Emil was known far and wide for his unwavering honesty and impeccable integrity. His character was shaped by the stories and teachings passed down through generations, tales that celebrated the virtues of truthfulness and accountability.

One fateful day, as Emil walked through the bustling marketplace, he stumbled upon a small pouch lying on the ground. Curiosity piqued, he picked it up and discovered that it contained a considerable sum of money. Emil's heart raced, and for a moment, the allure of wealth tempted him. But his upbringing and the wisdom of his ancestors whispered in his ear, reminding him of the values that defined his identity.

Filled with resolve, Emil set out to find the rightful owner of the pouch. He walked through the village, asking if anyone had lost a pouch of money. Days turned into weeks, and just as Emil was beginning to lose hope, he came across an elderly woman named Katarina. Tears streamed down her face as she recounted how she had lost her life savings, the very same pouch that Emil held in his hands.

Emil's heart swelled with compassion as he returned the pouch to Katarina. She clutched it tightly, gratitude etched across her weathered face. In that moment, a bond of trust and respect formed between them, a testament to the power of honesty and the impact of one's actions.

News of Emil's act of integrity spread like wildfire throughout the village and beyond. His tale became a symbol of the Romani community's commitment to honesty and honor. Romani elders shared the story with their children, ensuring that the lessons of truthfulness and accountability were passed down through the generations.

Emil's story is not a solitary one. Throughout history, there have been countless Romani individuals who have demonstrated unwavering honesty and integrity, leaving an indelible mark on our collective conscience. Their actions remind us of the importance of living a life guided by principles, even in the face of temptation or adversity.

One such figure is Ion Cioaba, a Romani king renowned for his commitment to justice and fairness. His reign was marked by his unwavering dedication to upholding the values of honesty and integrity within the Romani community. Ion's legacy serves as a reminder that leaders, too, can embody the virtues that shape a community's moral fabric.

The tale of Emil and the countless stories of honesty and integrity that grace our history teach us that our actions have consequences, not only for ourselves but also for those around us. They inspire us to uphold the principles of truthfulness and accountability, reminding us that our character and choices define us as individuals and as a community.

So, my dear listeners, let us carry the tale of Emil and the stories of honesty and integrity within our hearts. May they guide us in our own lives, reminding us of the importance of staying true to our values and the profound impact our actions can have on others. For in these stories, we find the eternal truth that honesty and integrity are the foundations upon which a noble and honorable life is built.

The Lesson of Respect and Equality

These narratives highlight the values of respect, inclusivity, and equality within the Romani community and beyond. They often revolve around situations where characters demonstrate respect for diversity, challenge prejudice and discrimination, and promote harmony among individuals from different backgrounds. Through these stories, moral teachings emphasize the importance of treating others with dignity and fairness. Below is a sample of such a story.

In the heart of a Romani village, nestled by the flowing river, there lived a wise elder named Sofia. Known for her profound wisdom and compassionate spirit, Sofia was a beacon of respect and equality within the community. She carried within her the stories and teachings that celebrated the values of diversity, inclusivity, and the intrinsic worth of every individual.

One day, a young Romani boy named Radu arrived in the village. Radu was different from the others - he hailed from a distant land and had a unique heritage that set him apart. Some villagers, blinded by their prejudices and biases, treated him with disdain and exclusion. But Sofia saw beyond these surface differences and recognized the richness that diversity brings.

With warmth and kindness, Sofia invited Radu to sit beside her by the fire. She shared tales of Romani heroes and heroines who had faced discrimination but triumphed against all odds. She spoke of individuals who stood up for justice, challenged prejudice, and embraced the value of every human being. Through these stories, Sofia taught Radu the importance of respect, inclusivity, and equality.

Inspired by Sofia's words, Radu found the strength within himself to rise above the negativity he encountered. He engaged with the other villagers, patiently educating them about his own culture and learning about theirs. Together, they celebrated their differences, recognizing that diversity was a source of strength rather than division.

Word of Sofia's teachings and the transformation in the village spread far and wide. Romani communities across the land started sharing their own stories, highlighting the importance of respect and equality. These stories showcased individuals who shattered stereotypes, challenged discrimination, and fostered a sense of harmony among diverse communities.

One such figure was Ceija Stojka, a Romani artist and writer who dedicated her life to promoting understanding and respect for Romani culture. Through her paintings and writings, she offered a glimpse into the rich heritage of the Romani people, breaking down stereotypes and fostering dialogue between different cultures. Ceija's work serves as a testament to the power of art and storytelling in promoting respect and equality.

The lessons of respect and equality within the Romani community extend beyond its borders. Romani individuals have long been at the forefront of social justice movements, fighting for the rights and dignity of marginalized groups. Their stories of resilience and activism inspire others to challenge prejudice, embrace diversity, and strive for a world where respect and equality are paramount.

So, my dear listeners, let us carry the lessons of respect and equality within our hearts. Let us embrace the diversity that enriches our lives, recognizing the inherent worth and value of every individual. Through our words and actions, may we challenge prejudice, promote inclusivity, and create a world where respect and equality flourish for all. For in these stories, we find the eternal truth that when we treat others with dignity and fairness, we cultivate a society built on compassion, harmony, and shared humanity.

Stories of Generosity and Compassion

These tales showcase acts of kindness, generosity, and compassion. They center around characters who selflessly help others in need, demonstrating the values of empathy, solidarity, and community support. In addition, the stories highlight the moral teachings of compassion, generosity, and the importance of helping those facing difficulties or adversity. Below is a sample of such a story.

In the heart of a Romani encampment, there lived a kind-hearted woman named Amara. She was known throughout the community for her boundless generosity and unwavering compassion. Amara possessed a deep understanding of the struggles faced by others and dedicated herself to making a positive impact on their lives.

One winter, a fierce snowstorm swept through the encampment, leaving many families in desperate need of warmth and shelter. Amara opened her doors and welcomed those in need, offering them a safe haven from the harsh elements. She distributed blankets, lit fires to warm cold hands, and shared what little food she had with a warm smile.

News of Amara's compassionate acts spread throughout the Romani community, and her humble dwelling became a refuge for those facing difficulties or adversity. People from far and wide sought solace in her presence, knowing that they would be met with open arms and a compassionate heart.

One day, a weary traveler named Andrei arrived at Amara's doorstep. Andrei had journeyed for miles, his heart heavy with sorrow. Amara sensed his pain and offered him a listening ear and a comforting embrace. As they shared stories and tears, Andrei discovered that he was not alone in his struggles. Amara's compassion and understanding reminded him of the power of human connection and the importance of helping others in their time of need.

Amara's acts of generosity and compassion were not limited to her own community. She traveled to neighboring villages, providing aid to those affected by natural disasters, poverty, or illness. Her selflessness inspired others to join her in acts of kindness, creating a ripple effect of compassion that extended far beyond the Romani encampment.

The stories of Romani generosity and compassion do not end with Amara. Throughout history, Romani individuals have extended a helping hand to those in need, regardless of their cultural background or ethnicity. Their acts of kindness have transcended borders, fostering a spirit of solidarity and unity.

One notable figure is Dr. Ian Hancock, a Romani scholar and activist who has dedicated his life to advocating for the rights of Romani people worldwide. His work in academia and social justice movements has shed light on the challenges faced by Romani communities and has fostered a greater understanding of their culture and history. Dr. Hancock's tireless efforts exemplify the values of generosity and compassion that run deep within the Romani tradition.

The stories of Romani generosity and compassion remind us of the power we hold to make a positive difference in the lives of others. They teach us that a simple act of kindness can brighten someone's day, provide comfort in times of distress, and restore hope in the face of adversity. Let us embrace the spirit of generosity and compassion, for in doing so, we uplift not only those around us but also our own souls. May these stories inspire us to extend a helping hand, lend a listening ear, and spread love and compassion wherever we go.

Cultural Wisdom

The Importance of Family and Community

These narratives emphasize the significance of family bonds, community support, and the interconnectedness of individuals within the Romani culture. They convey the values of unity, mutual assistance, and strength derived from collective identity. Through these stories, cultural wisdom is imparted, encouraging the preservation of family ties, and nurturing a strong sense of community. Below is a sample of such a story.

In a small Romani village nestled amidst picturesque landscapes, the importance of family and community was woven into the very fabric of daily life. The villagers understood that their strength and resilience lay not only in their individual endeavors but also in the unity and support of their tight-knit community.

One of the village elders, Sofia, would often gather the children around her to share stories of their ancestors and the significance of family ties. She recounted tales of Romani families who had endured countless hardships and challenges throughout history yet remained steadfast in their love and commitment to one another.

Sofia spoke of the Romani extended family structure, where grandparents, parents, aunts, uncles, and cousins formed an intricate web of support and guidance. She emphasized the role of elders as custodians of wisdom, passing down traditions, values, and cultural knowledge from one generation to the next.

These stories mirrored the reality of Romani communities, where multiple generations lived in close proximity, often sharing the same household or neighboring dwellings. The bonds forged within these extended families went beyond blood relations, embracing a sense of collective responsibility and care for one another.

In the village, community gatherings and celebrations were eagerly anticipated, as they offered moments of connection, solidarity, and shared joy. From lively weddings to festive holidays, every occasion was an opportunity to strengthen the ties that bound the community together.

The importance of community support was not limited to joyful times alone. In times of hardship, such as natural disasters or personal tragedies, the village rallied together to provide assistance and comfort. Whether it was rebuilding homes after a devastating storm or offering emotional support to those who had lost loved ones, the community stood as a pillar of strength for its members.

Historically, Romani communities have demonstrated the power of collective action in overcoming challenges. During times of persecution and discrimination, they formed tight-knit communities that offered refuge, protection, and a sense of belonging. The Romani tradition of "phralipe," or brotherhood, fostered a spirit of solidarity and mutual assistance that ensured the survival and resilience of the community.

One notable example of the strength of Romani family and community bonds is reflected in the life and work of Matéo Maximoff, a Romani writer and activist. Maximoff dedicated his writings and activism to preserving Romani culture and advocating for the rights of Romani people. He emphasized the importance of family ties, communal support, and the preservation of Romani traditions as crucial elements in fostering a sense of identity, pride, and resilience.

The stories of family and community within Romani culture remind us of the power of connection and mutual support. They teach us that we are stronger together, that our collective strength lies in the bonds we share with our loved ones and communities. Through these narratives, we are reminded to cherish and nurture our family ties, to extend a helping hand to those in need, and to cultivate a strong sense of belonging and unity. For it is within the embrace of family and community that we find the solace, strength, and enduring love that sustains us through life's journey.

Traditions and Celebrations

These tales revolve around cultural traditions, rituals, and celebrations that hold significance within Romani culture. They provide insights into the customs, practices, and beliefs that shape the fabric of Romani identity. These stories transmit cultural wisdom, ensuring that traditions are upheld, passed on to younger generations, and celebrated as an integral part of Romani heritage. Below is a sample of such a story.

Once upon a time, in the heart of our Romani village, nestled among the majestic Carpathian Mountains, there lived a community whose spirits danced to the rhythm of traditions and celebrations. These tales I weave for you today are not mere stories, but glimpses into our vibrant Romani culture, where customs, rituals, and festivities are intertwined with the very fabric of our identity.

Imagine, my dear listeners, the gathering of our Romani people at the annual Music Festival. As the sun dipped below the horizon, the village square became a stage of enchantment. The air filled with the soul-stirring melodies of violins, the pulsating beats of drums, and the harmonious whispers of accordions. Our talented Romani musicians, their fingers dancing across strings and keys, wove melodies that reached deep into the souls of all who listened.

And oh, the dancers! Adorned in the kaleidoscope of our traditional attire, they moved gracefully, their every step telling stories of our ancestors and the resilience that courses through our veins. Each twirl, each sway, carried the essence of our Romani spirit, a celebration of who we are, and a testament to the beauty that emerges when culture and rhythm become one.

But our celebrations go beyond music and dance, my dear friends. Our craftsmanship, honed over generations, takes center stage at our festivals. In every vibrant textile, in every hand-woven basket, in every delicate piece of jewelry adorned with gemstones, we infuse our cultural heritage. These creations are not mere objects; they are living reflections of our passion, our creativity, and the unbreakable thread that connects us to our ancestors.

Ah, and let me not forget the joyous union of love that is our Romani wedding. It is a celebration where the very air vibrates with excitement and unity. The bride and groom, dressed in attire that shines like the sun, exchange rings and coins, symbolic tokens of eternal commitment. It is a time when our community gathers, not just as guests, but as a family, to celebrate the sacred bond of marriage and the strength that lies in our deep-rooted customs.

And what is a celebration without food, my dear listeners? Our Romani feasts are a feast for all senses. The enticing aroma of lamb stew, the sizzle of stuffed peppers in the pan, and the mouthwatering taste of savory pastries create a symphony of flavors that bring smiles to our faces and warmth to our hearts. In the spirit of our hospitality, no one leaves the table hungry, for in our Romani culture, all are embraced as family.

Through the changing seasons, we mark the passage of time with our unique cultural and religious holidays. Romani Day, a vibrant festival of joy and togetherness, fills the air with laughter and celebration. And on St. George's Day, a day of reverence, we pay homage to our ancestors and honor the strength they bestowed upon us. These celebrations, dear friends, keep our spirits alive, connecting us to our past, grounding us in the present, and guiding us towards a future filled with hope.

These tales of our traditions and celebrations, handed down through generations, are not simply stories. They are the threads that weave our Romani tapestry, binding us together as a community, and reminding us of the beauty and resilience that flows through our veins. So let us cherish our customs, let us dance to the rhythm of our traditions, and let us pass on the flame of our Romani culture to future generations, for it is in celebrating who we are that our spirits truly soar.

The Wisdom of Elders

These narratives center around the wisdom and guidance of older generations within the Romani community. They showcase the respect and reverence given to elders as the bearers of cultural knowledge, experience, and wisdom. Through these stories, cultural wisdom is shared, highlighting the importance of listening to and learning from the wisdom of those who came before, fostering intergenerational understanding, and preserving the cultural legacy. Below is a sample of such a story.

Come, gather around the fire, dear ones, as I share with you the tales that carry the wisdom of our Romani elders. For in their eyes, lies the story of our people, the treasure trove of knowledge that illuminates our path and guides us through life's twists and turns.

In the heart of our Romani village, beneath the sprawling oak tree, sits the wise elder, his face etched with the lines of a life well-lived. His voice, a gentle melody, captivates all who listen, as he imparts the wisdom passed down from generation to generation. He speaks of honor, of resilience, and the power of our Romani spirit.

In these narratives, we learn that the wisdom of our elders is not confined to mere words; it is a living, breathing testament to the strength of our heritage. They share tales of their own journeys, of the challenges they faced, and the lessons they learned along the way. Through their stories, we discover the importance of perseverance, the value of community, and the beauty of embracing our unique Romani identity.

Our elders teach us the significance of respecting our traditions and honoring our ancestors. They remind us of the sacred rituals that bind us together, that carry the echoes of our past and the hopes of our future. They teach us the language of our people, the dances that tell our stories, and the songs that carry our spirits.

In the wisdom of our elders, we find a wellspring of guidance. They teach us the importance of family, the strength of unity, and the power of unconditional love. Their stories remind us of the values that form the foundation of our Romani culture - kindness, compassion, and the unwavering belief in the potential of every individual.

Through these narratives, we learn to listen, to truly hear the voices of our elders. Their wisdom is not to be taken lightly, for it is a gift that has been nurtured and refined over time. It is a torch passed from one generation to the next, lighting our way as we navigate the complexities of life.

So let us gather around the fire, dear ones, and listen to the wisdom of our elders. Let their stories weave a tapestry of understanding and connection, bridging the gap between the past and the present. For in their words, we find the keys to unlocking our true potential, to embracing our Romani heritage, and to creating a future that honors the wisdom of those who came before us.

The Fairytales

Once upon a time, an enchanting Romani community thrived amidst a world brimming with wonder and enigma. Their campfires flickered with tales that transcended the constraints of time, captivating the hearts of all who hearkened. These narratives reverberated across generations, carrying within them the profound wisdom, magical essence, and unyielding resilience of the Romani people.

In this assemblage of Romani fairy tales, we beckon you to embark on a mesmerizing odyssey into a realm where melodies harmonize with blossoming roses, mighty sons rise to confront extraordinary trials, and the veils of the universe unveil themselves to those blessed with a gypsy's discernment. Each story weaves an indelible testament to the enduring spirit and indomitable courage inherent in the Romani people.

The fairy tales presented in this volume find their origins in a work I have translated entitled *Cikánské Pohádky*, meticulously rendered by Zdenka Hostinska and initially published in 1913 by A.L. Hynek. In crafting this adaptation, I have striven to retain the core essence of each tale while contemporizing the language to resonate with modern readers.

Our journey commences with "The Rose and the Musician," a tale whisking us away to a realm where a humble minstrel unravels the transformative power of love as he endeavors to capture the heart of a princess. Will the enchanting melodies emanating from his enchanted violin prove potent enough to sway her affections?

Venturing deeper into the realm of ancient legends, we encounter "The Mighty Son of The King." This narrative chronicles the extraordinary exploits of a young prince endowed with unparalleled strength, embarking on a perilous quest to liberate his kingdom from the clutches of an evil sorcerer. Along his treacherous path, he encounters mythical creatures, tests the limits of his bravery, and unravels the true essence of heroism.

In "The Omniscient Gypsy," we encounter a sage elder within the Romani community, whose wisdom transcends the ordinary bounds of human perception. With clairvoyant abilities, this figure assumes the role of a beacon, guiding those in need and unraveling the enigmatic mysteries that shroud the cosmos, offering profound insights that shape the trajectories of lives.

Prepare to be transported to ethereal heights in "The Floating Mountain," an enchanting chronicle that unveils the captivating encounter of a young Romani girl with a mountain that defies the laws of gravity. Through her audacity and resourcefulness, she unveils the hidden powers concealed within this ethereal summit, while simultaneously discovering the paramount importance of safeguarding the wonders of nature.

However, be forewarned of the chilling tale that unfolds in "The Headless Rider," where a mysterious equestrian entity haunts the nightscape, engendering terror among all who dare cross its path. Will any soul muster the courage to confront this fearsome specter and unveil the truth that lingers behind its ominous presence?

The mystical allure of "The Three Magical Eggs" beckons us next, as three humble eggs unearth extraordinary wonders, bequeathing incredible gifts upon those fortunate enough to possess them. Yet, we must tread cautiously, for great power intertwines with profound responsibility.

Within the pages of "The Man with Five Heads," a world veiled in illusions and metamorphosis unfolds before our eyes. Join us on an exhilarating expedition as a cunning Romani traveler encounters an individual concealing an astonishing secret. Will he succeed in unraveling the enigma of the five heads while eluding the clutches of malevolent sorcery?

Concealed treasures lie in wait within "The Gypsy and The Treasure." Follow the intrepid footsteps of a spirited Romani traveler as she embarks on a treacherous pilgrimage in search of a legendary treasure. Along her arduous path, she confronts cunning traps, encounters mythical creatures, and tests the limits of her wit and courage. Will her unwavering determination lead her to the coveted prize, or will the journey itself become the true treasure, illuminating the profound lessons of resilience, perseverance, and self-discovery?

"The Seven Brothers and The Devil" unfolds a tale of profound brotherhood, unwavering loyalty, and the power of faith. When seven brothers make a fateful pact with the devil, their lives take an unexpected turn as they navigate a treacherous path toward wealth. Will their bond prove strong enough to withstand the temptations that lay ahead, or will they succumb to the sinister allure of their unholy agreement?

Prepare to be captivated by "The Man Without a Shadow," an extraordinary narrative that plunges us into a realm where a Romani man finds himself mysteriously devoid of a shadow. This inexplicable phenomenon propels him on a profound quest to unravel the meaning behind his existence. As he embarks on this introspective journey, he unravels the profound interplay between light and darkness, ultimately discovering the essence of being and the profound interconnectedness of all existence.

Finally, we delve into the depths of existential contemplation with "Nothingness." Within a world fixated on material possessions and external measures of worth, we encounter a man who embraces the very concept of nothingness. Through encounters with the enigmatic Mr. Nothing, he learns to find liberation within the intangible beauty of existence itself, unburdened by the weight of material accumulation. In this tale of philosophical introspection, we are invited to question our own perceptions of value and embrace the intrinsic wonders of human experience.

As you journey through this section of this book, prepare to be spellbound by a realm where Romani folklore intertwines with the boundless realms of imagination. These tales are not mere whimsical flights of fancy; they are profound reflections of life's complexities, offering timeless lessons, insights, and a poignant exploration of the human condition. May these Romani fairy tales illuminate the depths of your soul, leaving an indelible imprint that resonates with wisdom, compassion, and a renewed appreciation for the tapestry of human existence.

A Flower for Luck

Once upon a time, in a land far away, there lived an elderly mother and her only son. They dwelled in a small cottage and faced the harsh reality of poverty. As the mother approached the end of her life, she wept tears of sadness for her son's future. With a heavy heart, she spoke to him, "My dear son, it is time for you to explore the world and seek your happiness. Soon, I will pass away, and in this village, you will find no solace or kind words, for we are humble folk. But before I depart, promise me this: once I am laid to rest, come to my grave at the stroke of midnight and pluck the flower that will bloom upon it. Keep it close, for it shall serve as the guiding light on your path to happiness."

Sadly, the mother's time came to an end, and the son tenderly buried her. When darkness veiled the world, he made his way to the graveyard, and there, upon his mother's freshly dug grave, a wondrous blue flower blossomed. Gently, he plucked it and concealed it within his pocket.

The following day, the young man embarked on his journey, hoping to find the happiness his mother desired for him. As he traveled, he encountered a limping wolf in distress. With compassion in his heart, the young man approached the wolf and carefully removed a thorn from its paw. Grateful, the wolf spoke, "Though I cannot repay your kindness immediately, take a single hair from my fur. When the time comes, and you need my aid, simply breathe upon it." The young man plucked a hair from the wolf and placed it alongside the blue flower in his pocket.

Days turned into weeks, and weeks into months as the young man wandered tirelessly, searching for his elusive happiness. Yet, his journey seemed in vain. Then, he remembered his mother's words and retrieved the blue flower from his pocket. With a tinge of doubt, he placed it on the ground, and to his amazement, the flower levitated and spoke, "Follow me, for I am visible only to you. Fear not and come along, as I shall lead you to the path of your happiness."

Enchanted, the young man trailed behind the floating flower, following its ethereal glow. As twilight cast its golden hues upon the land, they arrived in a dense forest. Amidst the trees, a cunning fox appeared before him. The fox addressed him politely, "Kind sir, a mischievous wasp has found its way into my ear, causing me great discomfort. Could you please remove it for me?" Moved by the fox's plea, the young man carefully extracted the wasp, and in gratitude, the fox spoke with wisdom, revealing a secret, "In your pursuit of happiness, you must first serve under a wicked sorceress. Your task will be to lead a cow with golden horns to graze in the meadow. But beware, the cow must never return home without you, or the sorceress will unleash her dark powers upon you. If you succeed in keeping the cow in the pasture, ask for your reward—a cap hanging behind the stove. Wearing this cap will render you invisible to all." With these words, the fox disappeared, leaving the young man filled with anticipation. He securely grasped the blue flower, gently returning it to his pocket, and laid down to rest.

The following day, the young man retrieved the blue flower once more. It floated gracefully before him, guiding him with its enchanting presence. They arrived at an imposing iron house where an elderly woman, known as Baba, stood at the threshold. Her wrinkled face exuded an air of mystery as she questioned the young man, "What brings you to this place?" Humbly, the young man replied, "Dear lady, I seek employment and purpose." Baba nodded knowingly and granted him entry into her service. "Your task," she instructed, her voice laced with caution, "will be to lead the cow with golden horns to the lush pastures. But remember, the cow must never return home without you, or dire consequences shall befall you. However, should you succeed in tending to the cow for three days, you shall have the freedom to choose any item from my humble abode as your reward." The young man listened attentively, understanding the weight of his duty, as a sense of determination ignited within him.

Guided by the ethereal presence of the blue flower, the young man embraced his new responsibility. With each step, he marveled at the beauty of nature surrounding him, forging a deep connection with the majestic cow and its golden horns. They reached the verdant meadow, where the cow grazed contentedly. However, as the hours passed, restlessness overcame the cow, tempting her to return home. Sensing the urgency, the young man retrieved the wolf's hair and, with a gentle breath, summoned a pack of wolves from the depths of the forest. They encircled the cow, ensuring she remained in place, protected from straying away. As the sun dipped below the horizon, the young man guided the cow back to Baba's abode and settled into his bed, awaiting the dawn of a new day.

For three consecutive days, the young man repeated the routine, tending to the cow with unwavering dedication. On the third day, he returned to Baba with the cow, having successfully completed his task. Impressed by his loyalty, Baba granted him permission to explore her dwelling and choose his well-deserved reward. Amidst the treasures, his eyes fell upon a cap hanging discreetly behind the stove. With a sense of certainty, he reached out and claimed it, sensing its extraordinary power. However, as he held the cap in his hands, Baba erupted in anger, attempting to snatch it away. Swiftly, the young man placed the cap upon his head, becoming invisible to her grasp. With a triumphant smile, he stepped outside and removed the cap, hearing the gentle voice of the flower whispering, "Release me!" Complying with its plea, he gently freed the flower from his pocket, watching as it floated gracefully before him, emanating a sense of wonder and possibility.

Filled with renewed hope, the young man embarked on his continued journey, venturing through unfamiliar lands. Days turned into weeks, and weeks into months, as he encountered various challenges and obstacles. Yet, he pressed on, guided by the invisible flower, whose presence reassured him.

One day, as the young man grew weary, he arrived at the shores of a tranquil lake. The sun began its descent, casting a golden glow upon the rippling waters. Lying down on the shore, he embraced the peaceful surroundings. To his surprise, the flower spoke softly, "Place me in your pocket." Trusting its guidance, he tucked the flower away and settled beneath the shade of a nearby tree. With the moon shining brightly and illuminating the gray rocks of the mountains, the young man succumbed to a deep slumber.

In the depths of the night, a cry shattered the tranquility, jolting the young man from his peaceful rest. Startled, he looked around and witnessed a large toad gripping the leg of a tiny man, no taller than a couple of hand spans. Reacting swiftly, the young man hurled a stone at the toad, causing it to release its grip on the helpless creature. The little man scurried towards the young man, pleading, "Thank you for saving me! That toad is an evil sorceress in disguise, capable of summoning countless toads to harm us." With a sense of urgency, the young man swiftly retrieved his cap, placing it upon his head. Almost instantly, a multitude of toads appeared, searching for him but unable to perceive his presence. The young man and the little man continued their journey, united by a shared purpose and the invisible protection provided by the cap.

As the first rays of dawn peeked over the horizon, they arrived at a majestic cave nestled within the heart of the mountains. The little man spoke, "Set me down and follow my lead. I will guide you towards happiness and prosperity." Intrigued, the young man gently placed the little man on the ground, watching as he knocked three times on the rocky wall. "Open in the center, I bring a guest. Open swiftly, my brethren!" the little man proclaimed.

To their amazement, the doors of the cave swung open, revealing a hidden realm teeming with life. The little man turned to the young man and advised, "Conceal your cap so that my brothers may see you." The young man obeyed, tucking the cap away and stepping into a magnificent wooden room. Its walls exuded warmth and tranquility. From there, they proceeded to an iron room, where numerous iron bottles gleamed with an otherworldly sheen. The air was charged with an aura of strength and resilience. Finally, they opened another set of doors, leading them into a golden chamber adorned with jewels and precious metals. Many little men had gathered around their king, who stood just as small as the others, yet possessed a regal presence with his long, silver beard.

The little man led the young man to the king's side and spoke with reverence, "Most gracious king, this young man saved my life from the wicked sorceress, who had transformed into a toad, intending to harm me." The king's eyes sparkled with gratitude as he gazed upon the young man. "You have indeed shown great bravery and compassion," the king acknowledged. "In return, I shall bestow upon you gifts that will bring you lasting happiness."

With a graceful motion, the king plucked a single silver hair from his beard and handed it to the young man, saying, "When you find yourself in the depths of distress, but only then, breathe upon this hair, and I will come with my people to offer assistance." The young man accepted the precious gift with gratitude, securing it alongside the wolf's hair and the blue flower in his pocket.

The king then led his honored guest to a silver chamber, where a shimmering bottle awaited. He presented it to the young man, explaining, "This bottle contains water that shall never diminish. When you moisten a stone with this enchanted water, it will transform into pure gold." The young man marveled at the gift, his heart filled with wonder and gratitude.

Their journey within the cave continued as they returned to the iron room. The king reached for a finely crafted rifle and placed it in the young man's hands. "With this rifle, you will hit any target you aim for," the king proclaimed. "Now, my dear guest, it is time for you to depart our realm. No mortal should linger in our kingdom for too long."

Expressing his gratitude, the young man bid

farewell to the king and the little men, who had guided him on his path. Stepping out of the cave, he felt a renewed sense of purpose and determination. The blue flower, sensing his readiness, cried out, "Release me!" The young man then gently freed the blue flower from his pocket, allowing it to float before him once again. It emanated a soft, ethereal glow, guiding him onwards.

Days turned into weeks as the young man journeyed through unfamiliar lands, his heart filled with hope and the companionship of the invisible flower. Along the way, he encountered various trials and tribulations, yet he pressed on, unwavering in his pursuit of happiness.

Finally, his path led him to a breathtaking mountain range, with towering peaks piercing the sky. Weary from his travels, the young man found solace in the shade of a majestic tree. As he rested, the blue flower whispered softly, "Place me in your pocket." Trusting its guidance, he carefully tucked the flower away, its gentle presence a comforting reminder of his mother's love.

With the blue flower leading the way, the young man continued his journey through the vast and unknown lands. Days turned into weeks, and weeks into months, as he encountered trials and obstacles along his path. Yet, he persevered, guided by the invisible flower and the gifts bestowed upon him.

Finally, he arrived at a breathtaking glass cliff, where the world seemed to shimmer and reflect like a mirage. As he gazed upon the cliff's edge, the flower urged him to prepare himself for the challenge that lay ahead.

With a steady heart, the young man approached the edge of the cliff, ready to face the guardian of the beautiful maidens who resided there. He called upon the power of the king's silver hair, breathing upon it with determination. In an instant, the air stirred, and a legion of little men, led by the king himself, materialized beside him.

"The time has come," the king declared, his voice filled with authority. "We shall lend our strength to aid you in your noble quest."

With their collective might, they charged forward, engaging in a fierce battle with the dragon guarding the maidens. The young man, armed with the rifle bestowed upon him, unleashed his precise aim, striking the dragon with unwavering accuracy. The dragon, no match for their combined forces, disintegrated into dust and smoke, vanishing into the wind.

As the dust settled and victory was achieved, a sense of joy and relief washed over the young man. The blue flower, now glowing with radiant light, whispered, "Farewell, my child. I am the spirit of your departed mother, and now I shall return to the heavens from whence I came."

With a mix of emotions, the young man bid farewell to the blue flower, forever grateful for its guidance and protection throughout his journey. He felt a profound sense of accomplishment and purpose as he turned his attention to the maidens who had been freed from the dragon's clutches.

Among the maidens, the young man found the youngest sister, the one he had saved at the lake with the golden geese. Their eyes met, and in that instant, a deep connection blossomed between them. Love sparked within their hearts, and they knew they were destined to be together. The young man and the maiden embraced, celebrating their newfound happiness and the triumph over adversity.

In the days that followed, the other two sisters also found their perfect matches, bringing even more joy and harmony to their lives. United in love and gratitude, they returned to the young man's homeland, where they built a prosperous and joyful life together.

Their home became a haven of love, filled with laughter, wealth, and contentment. The gifts bestowed upon the young man by the king and the spirits of his mother continued to bless their lives, bringing prosperity and abundance.

The golden cow grazed in their meadows, and the stones transformed into gleaming gold at the touch of the enchanted water. The young man's aim remained true with the magical rifle, ensuring their safety, and providing for their every need.

The king's silver hair became a symbol of hope and reassurance, serving as a reminder that assistance was only a breath away in times of distress. And the cap, when worn upon their heads, granted them the gift of invisibility, allowing them to navigate through the world unseen when necessary.

As the years passed, their love grew deeper, and their happiness knew no bounds. They shared their wealth and wisdom with those in need, spreading kindness and compassion throughout the land.

Their story, a tale of bravery, perseverance, and the power of love, echoed through generations. It became a cherished fairy tale, passed down from parent to child, reminding them of the extraordinary possibilities that await those who dare to venture into the unknown and follow the guiding light of their hearts.

And so, the young man, his beloved wife, and her sisters lived a life filled with love, joy, and the magic that had accompanied them on their remarkable journey. They stood as a testament to the power of resilience and the rewards that come to those who embrace the call of adventure and never lose faith in the pursuit of happiness.

The Rose and the Musician

Once upon a time, there was a king and queen who lived in happiness and contentment. However, their marriage remained childless, which saddened the queen and disappointed the king. Determined to find a solution, the queen sought guidance from an old woman skilled in magical arts. She pleaded with the old woman for advice, and the old woman responded, "This is a difficult matter. If you desire a daughter, I can guide you, but you will never bear a son.

On the night of Good Friday, go alone to the cemetery before midnight, dig up the bone of a hanged man, and bring it home. On the first Easter holiday, grind the bone into powder. Then, take a strand of hair from a girl who is seven years, seven months, seven weeks, and seven days old. Add the hair to the powder and boil it with seeds from maiden apples in a new pot. Eat the porridge, and you will give birth to a daughter." The queen followed the old woman's instructions and gave birth to a beautiful rose, which flew out of the open window and became entangled in a rose bush.

In haste, the king and his servants rushed to the garden, hoping to pluck the rose from the bush. However, their efforts were in vain, as no one could retrieve it. Filled with rage, the king confronted his wife, accusing her of being a witch and decreeing that she must leave the kingdom immediately or face death.

The sick queen was forced to leave her bed and be exiled from the land. She found solace in the garden near the rose, where she sat and wept while kissing her rosy child. A dewdrop glistened in the calyx of the rose, and a voice spoke, "Do not cry, mother! Drink the dewdrop that shines in my calyx, and you will always find food and drink whenever you need it."

The queen followed her rosy daughter's advice and left the kingdom. After a long journey, she came upon a forest and discovered a spacious cave. She decided to make it her home, seeking solitude away from people. Each morning when she woke up, she found the most exquisite food and drinks awaiting her. The wild animals in the forest never harmed her; instead, they would come with their cubs, dancing and playing, bringing laughter and joy to the once unhappy queen. Birds sang their most beautiful songs, and exquisite flowers grew abundantly around her cave. In this way, the poor queen lived in the forest for a long time, unaware of the events unfolding with the king and her rosy daughter.

Years passed, and the rose in the king's garden continued to bloom year after year, in all seasons. The king, often captivated by its beauty, would approach the rose. However, as he drew near, the rose would close its calyx and droop on its stem, leaving the king saddened. One day, as the king stood before the rose, feeling despondent, he quietly pondered aloud, "If only I knew why the rose withers whenever I approach!" To his surprise, a voice responded, "You banished my mother from the land, leaving her to live on the outskirts in a cave. If you bring my mother back home, I will no longer wither in your presence."

Determined to right his wrongs, the king sent his people far and wide to search for the queen and bring her back. Eventually, several servants found the queen in her cave and returned her to the king. With the queen's return, joyful life resumed in the royal household. The rose bloomed more beautifully than ever before and no longer withered when the king approached. News of the royal daughter and the miraculous 'rose spread far and wide throughout the kingdoms. People from distant lands came to witness the wonder of the flower. Lords and kings arrived, bearing precious gifts, hoping to aid in the restoration of the rose's human form. However, despite their efforts, the rose remained steadfast on its bush, refusing to transform.

Desperate for a solution, the king consulted both good and evil sorcerers, promising them great rewards if they could restore the rose to its human shape. However, none of their spells and incantations proved successful. The king grew disheartened, fearing that his daughter would forever remain a rose.

One day, a humble musician arrived at the king's garden. From the window, the king and queen observed him and heard his words, "Oh, what a beautiful rose! I must at least kiss it, for I cannot pick it!" Moved by his words, the musician leaned forward, kissed the rose gently, and then sat down beside it, playing a melancholic tune on his violin.

To the astonishment of all, including the king and queen, the rose responded to the musician's music. Its petals began to unfold, revealing a radiant maiden within. The musician and the maiden embraced, exchanging a tender kiss. The maiden spoke with gratitude, saying, "If someone had played like this before, I would have regained my human form much earlier."

The king, the queen, and all the people in the realm rejoiced at the miraculous transformation. The musician, now hailed as a hero, remained in the kingdom and married the royal daughter, whom he affectionately called his golden rose. Their love blossomed, and they lived happily ever after.

From that day forward, the kingdom celebrated the power of music and the enchanting tale of the rose and the musician. The rose, forever a symbol of resilience and hope, continued to bloom in the royal garden, reminding all who beheld it of the extraordinary journey it had undertaken. And so, the story of the royal daughter and the musician became a cherished legend, passed down through generations as a testament to the

transformative power of love and the magic
that resides within music.

The Mighty Son of The King

Once upon a time, in a land far away, there lived a king who had a beautiful queen whom he loved dearly. They ruled their kingdom with kindness and grace. But their happiness was overshadowed by the fact that they were childless. The queen longed for a child, and her wish was finally granted when she became pregnant.

To their astonishment, the queen gave birth to a hairy boy who possessed incredible strength from the moment he entered the world. He could run and talk as soon as he was born, and his strength was unmatched. News of the hairy boy's remarkable abilities spread throughout the kingdom, reaching even the king's ears.

However, instead of embracing his son with joy, the king was filled with anger and disappointment. He believed that a proper heir should not be hairy, and he saw the boy as a blemish on his royal lineage. In a fit of rage, the king ordered his servants to take the queen and the child deep into the forest, intending to have them killed and bring their hearts as proof.

The servants reluctantly followed the king's orders and led the queen and the boy into the forest. As they were about to carry out their gruesome task, the boy pleaded with them to allow his mother to pray in a nearby cave. The servants, moved by the boy's request, granted him this final moment with his mother.

As the queen entered the cave, the boy whispered to her, "No matter what happens, stay in the cave and wait for me." With those words, he turned and faced the servants who intended to end their lives. They lunged at him with their knives, but the boy remained calm. He allowed them to stab him, jumping and laughing as if unaffected by the pain. With each strike, he retaliated with his immense strength, overpowering the servants until they lay defeated.

Having dispatched his adversaries, the boy went to the cave where his mother awaited him. She was in tears, fearing for their lives. But the boy reassured her, "Do not cry, dear mother! We will stay here in this cave, and I will ensure that no harm comes to us."

True to his words, the hairy boy transformed the cave into a comfortable dwelling, a sanctuary where they would be safe from any danger. He then ventured into the surrounding forest, using his strength to gather provisions for their sustenance.

As time went by, the boy became known throughout the land for his extraordinary abilities and his benevolent nature. He would visit the nearby town, where the townspeople were initially afraid of his power. But soon they came to appreciate his kindness and generosity. The boy would request bread and pastries from the bakers and merchants, and in return, he would provide them with the necessary means to survive.

However, the people grew weary of the boy's actions. They felt oppressed and complained to the king about their suffering. Enraged, the king ordered his entire army to eliminate the hairy boy once and for all.

When the soldiers approached the cave, the boy instructed his mother to seek refuge inside while he confronted the army outside. With determination in his eyes, he shouted, "What do you want here?" The soldiers, instead of answering, responded with gunfire.

Undeterred, the boy exclaimed, "Now you're even spitting at me, you scoundrels!" He hurled enormous stones at the soldiers, their size and force overwhelming them. Many soldiers fell, unable to withstand the hairy boy's unmatched strength.

As the soldiers pressed forward, attempting to remove the rope encircling the dwelling, they became stuck, trapped by an invisible force. The boy had acquired a rope with a protective enchantment, preventing anyone from entering the enclosed space.

Defeating the soldiers, the hairy boy sent one survivor back to the king with a message. The survivor tremblingly delivered the news of the army's defeat and the extraordinary power possessed by the hairy boy. The king, realizing the futility of further aggression, began to consider a different approach.

Deeply troubled by the loss of his soldiers and the havoc caused by his actions, the king desired to make amends. He understood that the hairy boy's strength was a force to be reckoned with, and he sought to find a resolution that would ensure peace in his kingdom.

Word spread far and wide that the hairy boy had become a young man, still blessed with immense strength. People whispered of his kindness and the protection he offered to those in need. Amidst these rumors, a beautiful but impoverished girl came forward, willing to undertake a daunting task.

The girl approached the king, her eyes filled with determination. She expressed her desire to eat the hair of the hairy boy, believing that this act could be the key to his transformation. The king, intrigued by her bravery and willingness to help, summoned his son and the girl's request was granted.

The hairy boy, accompanied by his mother, had his hair cut by the queen herself. She carefully ground the hair into a fine powder and baked it into a cake. With hope in her heart, the poor girl consumed the cake, not knowing what the future held.

As soon as the cake disappeared, a remarkable

change took place. The hairy boy transformed before their eyes into a handsome young man, his hair no longer a symbol of otherness but a testament to his unique strength and character.

A wave of joy washed over the kingdom as the news of the miraculous transformation spread. The queen, in her generosity, forgave her husband for his past actions, understanding the trials they had all endured. The king, remorseful and humbled, pledged to support the union between his son and the girl who had brought about this wondrous change.

The young couple, now united in love and strength, became a symbol of hope and resilience for the entire kingdom. With his unmatched abilities, the hairy boy-turned-man fearlessly protected the land from any external threats, ensuring the safety and well-being of all its inhabitants.

And so, they lived happily and contentedly, their days filled with laughter, love, and the knowledge that sometimes true strength lies not in appearances but in the purity of the heart. The kingdom flourished under their reign, guided by compassion and a shared vision of harmony.

The tale of the hairy boy and the girl who ate his hair became a beloved legend passed down through generations. It reminded the people that true beauty can be found in the unlikeliest of places and that acts of courage and kindness can bring about extraordinary transformations.

And thus, the fairy tale of the hairy boy and his remarkable journey serves as a timeless reminder that strength, resilience, and love can conquer even the greatest of challenges, and that sometimes, the most extraordinary stories emerge from the most unexpected beginnings.

The Omniscient Gypsy

Once upon a time, there was a Gypsy who couldn't make a living at home and decided to venture into the world. Bidding farewell to his neighbors, he set out on his journey. By evening, he reached a forest and, tired, lay down under a tree. As he lay there, pondering where to go and how to earn an honest living, he suddenly heard a voice calling, "Come here to me!" He looked up and saw a small bird above him. Quickly, he climbed up the tree and caught the bird. When he climbed back down, the creature spoke, saying, "Dear man, please be kind and kill me. Bury my body under this tree but eat my heart and you will understand what others think of you." The Gypsy slaughtered the bird, ate its heart, and dug a small hole to bury its body. Once he had finished, he found a note that read, "If you want to be happy, return here in a year!" He buried the little body and lay down.

The next day, he continued his journey and arrived in a town. He was surprised to see everyone he encountered, both well-dressed ladies and gentlemen, crying. Since they all appeared well-off, he didn't dare to approach them and inquire about the cause of their sorrow. After wandering through the town for a while, he came across an old man who was also quietly weeping. Seeing the Gypsy, the old man thought to himself, "How fortunate he is! He is the only one not crying!" The Gypsy understood this immediately because he had the bird's heart untouched in his stomach. He asked the old man, "Kind sir, please tell me, why is everyone in this town crying?" The old man replied, "The inhabitants of this town are in great distress.

Nine years ago, a powerful dragon threatened to destroy our town and kill all its people. We made a deal with the dragon, promising to give him an eighteen-year-old maiden every year. Yesterday, we had to deliver the king's daughter to him, and he transformed her into a bird and flew away with her." The Gypsy inquired, "Can't you kill the dragon?"

The old man replied, "That is not so easy, my son! Twenty-nine of our bravest men fought the dragon, but he overpowered and killed them all. Only someone who can do something the dragon cannot be able to defeat him."

The Gypsy listened attentively and said after a while, "If that's the case, I am ready to find your dragon and overcome him."

Skeptically, the old man shook his head and said, "I don't believe it. But if you're determined to try, I will take you to our gracious king so that he can hear what you have in mind." They both went to the king, who sat in his chamber, weeping.

Upon hearing the Gypsy's intention, he said, "Twenty-nine of my best men were defeated in battle against the dragon, and you want to face him? However, if you're determined to do so, I will provide you with everything you need for your journey." He ordered the Gypsy to be equipped with fine attire, a horse, money, a rifle, and a sword.

However, the Gypsy declined the rifle and sword, saying, "Those would be of little help to me!" He dressed in beautiful clothes, tucked away the money, mounted the horse, and rode in the direction where the dragon resided.

On the eleventh day, in the morning, the Gypsy arrived at the iron castle of the dragon, who happened to be lying by the window, gazing out.

"What are you doing here, you worm?" The dragon roared with such a terrible voice that the Gypsy and his horse were knocked down. After struggling to get back on his feet, the Gypsy said to the dragon, "Behave more politely towards your guests, or it might not end well for you. Well, if you want to know why I have come, I will tell you, for I see that you are truly strong and mighty. I am the strongest and wisest man in the world, and I want to challenge you."

"Is that so?" replied the dragon. "You want to challenge me? Well then, prove your strength and roar so loudly that I collapse to the ground."

"I won't do that," said the Gypsy. "I don't want your house, which I find appealing, to collapse and bury you. And I won't exert myself without the prospect of a reward."

"Just wait, little one," the dragon roared. "I will come down to you immediately, and then it will be shown who is more capable between us."

And he approached the Gypsy, whose heart pounded loudly in his chest at the sight of the terrifying dragon. "Well then," said the dragon, "if you want to measure yourself against me, come, and I will show you my best tricks so that we don't waste any time. If you can do more than me, I will lose all my strength and weaken to the point where you could easily kill me."

They then went into the mountains, where the dragon would throw hundred-pound stones into the air so high that they couldn't even be seen, and then caught them as if they were balls. "That's very impressive," said the Gypsy after a while. "If the stones were made of gold, I would also throw them, but I don't play with ordinary, dirty stones."

"Today, I will show you my best tricks, and tomorrow you will show me what you can do," said the dragon, leading the Gypsy to the shore of a lake so vast that no human eye could see its end. "Pay attention," said the dragon. He lay flat on the ground, leaned over, and drank the entire lake, causing the fish to flop on the dry land. Then he spewed the water back into the lake and said, "Let's continue!"

He led the Gypsy to an infinitely long meadow, scattered virgin apple seeds there, and spat on the ground three times. From each seed grew an iron man. There were so many iron men that not even a blade of grass could be seen. They all rushed at the dragon, who struck each one on the head, causing them to vanish into the ground without a trace.

The dragon asked the Gypsy, "Well, how do you like my tricks?"

The Gypsy replied, "Drinking up a lake is not a masterful trick. When I was still very young, I drank up a lake twice as big, filled with wine, and I didn't even get drunk. And the iron men! Oh my, that's nothing! Last year, when I visited my uncle on the moon, I devoured three thousand dragon kings in just half an hour."

And the dragon became frightened and thought it would be better if he didn't dare to fight this man and instead killed him while he slept at night. The Gypsy immediately knew and said, "Listen! I will show you a masterful trick that you cannot do. Do you want me to tell you what you were just thinking about me?"

"Well, what was I thinking?"

"That you wanted to kill me tonight."

The dragon was startled, trembling all over, and said, "Yes, you're right, I was thinking that."

Then it occurred to him that the Gypsy was a devilish fellow who could do more than he could. And the Gypsy said again, "Now you thought that I was a devilish fellow and could do more than you."

The dragon jerked as if struck by lightning, believing that his end was near. The Gypsy said, "Now you thought that your end was near, and you are not mistaken."

He took a club and killed the dragon, who had weakened like a little child. He cut off the creature's talons, placed them in his bag, and was about to leave when suddenly thunder roared and lightning flashed, and eight beautiful maidens approached the Gypsy. They were the maidens who had been sacrificed to the dragon. They were all there, except for the ninth one, the king's own daughter.

When they kissed the Gypsy and thanked him for their liberation, they all set out on the journey, and on the eleventh day, they reached their hometown. Great joy filled the air, and all the people praised and rewarded the Gypsy, except for the king, who was sad and gloomy because his daughter was missing.

However, she had been transformed into a bird by a kind sorceress so that the dragon could not harm her. And when the Gypsy returned to the place after a year, where he had buried the slain bird, he found a beautiful princess, the king's daughter, sitting under the tree. He was overjoyed and immediately brought her back to her father, the king.

The king and all the people in the town were ecstatic, but the princess remained indifferent to it all. It saddened the king and everyone who knew her, and the Gypsy realized that the princess had no heart because he still had it in his stomach. Through an artificial means, he retrieved the heart from his stomach, and the princess ate it. From that day on, she rejoiced and cared for others like everyone else.

Because her heart had been in the Gypsy's stomach for so long, she fell in love with him and begged him to marry her. And so it happened, and the Gypsy lived long and happily with the king's daughter, and if he did not die, he is still alive today.

And thus, the Gypsy's journey from a wandering soul to a hero and beloved husband brought prosperity and joy to the kingdom. The people celebrated their love and the triumph over the dragon, forever grateful to the brave Gypsy who had changed their lives. And they all lived happily ever after, cherishing the lessons of compassion, bravery, and the power of love that had unfolded in their extraordinary tale.

The Floating Mountain

Once upon a time, in a distant land, there lived a young and poor Gypsy. Dissatisfied with his life in the tribe, he made a decision to embark on a journey into the unknown world. With his skills in tending to cauldrons and knowledge of blacksmithing, he believed he could make a living outside the confines of his tribe. And so, he set off on his grand adventure.

The young Gypsy traveled from town to town, from village to village, seeking work and opportunities. When he had no money, he walked the streets, calling out, "Cauldrons for rent, cauldrons!" Sometimes he found enough work to sustain himself for a few days, but as time passed, he became a wanderer, drifting from place to place.

One fateful day, he arrived at a vast and majestic mountain range. As he wandered through the towering peaks, he encountered an old man, wise and weathered by time. The old man looked at the Gypsy and said, "You possess the skills of a blacksmith. Today, I

will provide you with work. You shall shoe
my twelve horses."

Intrigued by the opportunity, the Gypsy
followed the old man to his home, perched
high on a hill. Standing before the horses, the
old man called out their names:

"Leo,
Ale,
Penelo,
Selo,
Kelo,
Kerelo,
Daro,
Faro,
Harulo,
Zino,
Rino,
Virulo!

Come forth swiftly, my loyal companions!"

And as if by magic, twelve magnificent black
horses appeared before the Gypsy. He was
filled with awe as he realized that these horses
possessed the ability to speak like humans.
The old man entrusted the Gypsy with a bag

filled with horseshoes, instructing him to shoe each of the horses.

As the old man retired into his house, one of the horses spoke to the Gypsy. With a touch of longing in its voice, it said, "Oh, how I wish we could regain our human forms!" Curiosity piqued, the Gypsy inquired, "Were you once humans?" The horse nodded and began to recount a tale of twelve brothers who lived happily with their beautiful sister in their homeland.

The horse continued, revealing that their peaceful existence was shattered when the old man arrived, seeking their sister's hand in marriage. Refusing his request, the brothers found themselves transformed into horses, banished to the mountains. Their sister, however, was imprisoned within a glass mountain.

Eager to help, the Gypsy asked how they could reclaim their human forms. The horse explained that their sister must be freed from her glass prison. But the horse, cautious of the sorcerer's return, warned the Gypsy to hide four horseshoes in his pocket. These enchanted horseshoes held the power to reveal secrets and allow horses to speak like humans.

With the four horseshoes safely stowed away, the Gypsy bid farewell to the old man and continued on his journey. Soon, he arrived at a bustling city, weary and hungry. Sitting on a stone near the city gates, he wished for a taste of good food from the bag. To his delight, the bag provided him with a feast fit for a king.

As he savored his meal, the Gypsy contemplated his next endeavor — acquiring a worthy horse. He reasoned that if he wished for money, the bag would grant his desire. But the sorcerer's warning echoed in his mind, cautioning against wishing for something living. Determined to find a solution, he decided to obtain a horse with extraordinary abilities, one that could guide him out of poverty.

Resisting the temptation to make a wish, the Gypsy instead uttered the words, "I wish..." But before he could complete his sentence, a strange smoke began to rise from the bag. To his astonishment, a magnificent black horse materialized before him. The horse spoke, its voice filled with wisdom, "You have chosen wisely. The bag remains, but here I stand. I am one of the twelve brothers, transformed into horses by the sorcerer. Mount me, and we shall fly swiftly to rescue our sister."

With a sense of excitement and anticipation, the Gypsy climbed onto the horse's back. As if propelled by the wind itself, they soared through the sky, traversing great distances in mere moments. Their destination was a vast lake, its tranquil surface disturbed by a mountain that spun tirelessly in its center. Perched atop the mountain was a small cottage where the beautiful maiden, the sister of the twelve horses, was imprisoned.

As they approached the lake, the Gypsy expressed his concern about crossing the scorching waters. The horse reassured him, saying that even if he could swim, the lake's heat was so intense that it could burn anything it touched to ashes. Their only chance was to obtain holy water.

Guided by the horse, they sought out a wise and benevolent priest who provided them with the sacred water. Equipped with this precious resource, they returned to the lake, ready to face the challenges ahead. The horse advised the Gypsy to fashion a small boat using one of the enchanted horseshoes from his pocket. Into this vessel, they poured the holy water.

Before embarking on the treacherous journey across the lake, the horse requested a sip of the holy water. As it drank, a remarkable transformation occurred. The horse's equine form faded away, replaced by a handsome young man standing before the Gypsy. With joy in his voice, the young man declared, "Once again, I have reclaimed my human form!"

Together, they kindled a fire and set to work forging the horseshoes into a sturdy boat. With their vessel prepared and filled with holy water, they embarked on their perilous voyage towards the spinning mountain.

Reaching the mountain's peak, the young man sprinkled the holy water upon it. In an awe-inspiring spectacle, the mountain shattered and dissolved, leaving behind a breathtaking sight. Standing in its place was the beautiful maiden, surrounded by eleven transformed brothers, now handsome young men. The joy of their reunion was immeasurable, and the Gypsy felt his heart fill with warmth.

United once again, the siblings expressed their profound gratitude to the Gypsy for his invaluable assistance. As time passed, the Gypsy and the beautiful maiden developed a deep bond, their hearts entwined in love. In a grand celebration, they were wed and embarked on a life filled with happiness and contentment.

The horse, now returned to its human form, revealed its extraordinary knowledge. With its guidance, the Gypsy and his new family unearthed hidden treasures and acquired great wealth, banishing all traces of poverty from their lives.

And so, they lived harmoniously, blessed with prosperity and the enduring love that had blossomed between the Gypsy and the maiden. Their story became a legend, shared through the generations, a tale of courage, loyalty, and the transformative power of love.

And if you ever find yourself wandering the world, seeking adventure or solace, remember this tale and the lessons it imparts. For within the humblest of souls lies the potential for extraordinary journeys and the fulfillment of dreams.

The Headless Rider

Once upon a time, there was a young, poor Gypsy who worked as a horse shepherd for a wealthy lord. He had the responsibility of tending to the horses day and night on the vast plains. The Gypsy was diligent in his work, but his heart yearned for something more.

One day, while leading the horses to graze, he stumbled upon a place he had never been before. To his amazement, it was a land of lush grass and flowing water, a paradise for the horses. Overwhelmed with excitement, he hurried back to his master and exclaimed, "Sir, I have discovered a marvelous pasture! The grass is abundant, and the water is pure. I wish to stay there as long as the horses need to graze."

The lord, taken aback, responded, "You won't last there for long. I have never had a shepherd who could endure more than a day and a night in that place." Curiosity sparked within the shepherd, and he questioned, "But why can't I stay longer than a day and a night?" With a cryptic smile, the lord simply said, "You will see," and walked away.

The poor shepherd returned to his herd; his mind consumed by the lord's enigmatic words. Evening descended, and weariness washed over him. As he lay down to rest, the stillness of the night was shattered by howling dogs gathering around him. The horses, sensing an otherworldly presence, huddled together, trembling in the meadow.

Suddenly, a thunderous uproar filled the air, and a horse galloped towards the shepherd. Astonishingly, the rider held his own severed head in his hand. The horse and its headless rider halted before the bewildered shepherd, and the head, with an eerie voice, asked, "What brings you to my pasture?" Startled but composed, the shepherd replied, "I seek the same as you, for it is a place of solace." The head, impressed by the shepherd's response, declared, "You have a sharp wit, young one. I am intrigued by your presence."

The shepherd, not one to back down, boldly stated, "I believe you, for they have severed your head." The head nodded sorrowfully and confessed, "Yes, I am condemned to wander without my body until someone can break the curse that binds me." Intrigued by the tragic tale, the shepherd implored, "tell me, who cursed you? Share your story with me." The head, overcome with grief, shed tears and began its tale, "I was once a wealthy man, living a life of peace and contentment.

One day, a priest approached me, seeking funds for the construction of a church that the villagers desired. Generously, I donated a considerable sum, and the priest departed. Later, I arrived in a village where the church was being built. For reasons unknown, I found myself among the crowd and uttered, 'Why build churches when the fields await? If God desires temples, let Him construct them Himself!' The enraged priest cast a curse upon me, and since then, I have roamed without a head, seeking redemption. Only when green leaves sprout from this staff will I find salvation." With those words, the headless rider handed the shepherd a dried staff, the symbol of their shared destiny.

Filled with determination, the shepherd declared, "With God's divine assistance, all things are possible. I shall pray for your redemption." He planted the staff firmly in the ground and began fervently praying. As dawn broke, a miraculous sight unfolded before their eyes. Green leaves burst forth from the staff, signifying the shepherd's unwavering faith and the imminent release of the cursed rider. In that transformative moment, the headless rider's neck became whole again, and the severed head miraculously reattached itself.

A surge of joy and relief washed over them both. Overwhelmed with gratitude, the now-reunited man and horse realized that their destinies had intertwined. The headless rider revealed himself as a benevolent spirit, longing to repay the shepherd's kindness. "You have freed me from my curse," he said, "and now I shall repay you with love and protection. Come with me to my dwelling, and you shall become my son and heir. Together, we will embark on a new journey."

The once-poor shepherd, now embraced by the spirit as his own, eagerly accepted the offer. They traveled to a magnificent house, where the spirit assumed the role of a wise and devoted priest, serving the very God he had once offended. The shepherd thrived under the guidance of his newfound father, learning the ways of faith, compassion, and the teachings of their shared religion.

In time, the shepherd's humble origins faded into the background as he grew in wealth and prosperity. His wisdom and generosity echoed the spirit's teachings, spreading throughout the community. The once-wealthy man, now a priest, dedicated himself to the service of God, humbled by his past mistakes and striving to bring peace and harmony to those around him.

Together, the shepherd and the priest brought blessings and goodwill to the land. Their bond grew stronger with each passing day, uniting their hearts as family. The house flourished with laughter, love, and spiritual guidance. The shepherd, once burdened by poverty and uncertainty, now reveled in the joy and abundance that life had bestowed upon him.

And so, the tale of the poor shepherd and the headless rider became a testament to the transformative power of faith, compassion, and the capacity for redemption. Their story inspired generations to seek understanding, forgiveness, and the belief that even the most shattered souls can find healing and purpose.

In the end, the shepherd and the priest left behind a legacy of love, grace, and the enduring reminder that in the realm of miracles, no curse is too great to be lifted and no soul too lost to be redeemed. Their tale continues to be told, reminding all who hear it of the boundless possibilities that lie within the human spirit and the profound connections that can be forged amidst the most extraordinary circumstances.

The Three Magical Eggs

Once upon a time, there lived a young and impoverished Romani boy. Within a week, he tragically lost his parents and his beloved. With a heavy heart, he buried them, but his poverty prevented him from arranging a funeral feast. Living day by day, barely making ends meet, he struggled to cope with his grief.

One night, a week after the burial, he was awakened by the sensation of his tent being shaken. Startled, he asked, "Who's there?" and to his astonishment, he heard his father's voice lamenting, "You buried me without giving me any milk." The following night, the same shaking and questioning occurred, and this time it was his mother's voice reproaching him for not providing any milk in her burial. And on the subsequent night, his lover's voice echoed the same grievance. Overwhelmed with sorrow, he stepped out of his tent into the darkness, unable to see anything but the haunting voices of his loved ones.

His lover's voice, barely audible, whispered a solution to bring them peace. "If you seek to bring us tranquility, go up into the mountains. In a cave, you will find three eggs. Take them with you and try to open them, though the path to reach them will not be easy." And with those words, the spirit of his beloved disappeared into the night.

The next morning, at the break of dawn, the young Romani boy embarked on his journey. High up in the mountains, he encountered an elderly woman struggling to carry a large sack on her back. Moved by compassion, he offered to carry the sack for her. Curiously, he found the burden surprisingly light and inquired about its contents. The old woman revealed that it contained the souls of stillborn children, destined for the realm of the dead.

They continued their arduous climb until they reached a cave, where the old woman declared their arrival. The boy, taken aback by the swift journey, asked about the speed, to which the old woman explained that time passes differently in the realm of the dead. Although they had yet to enter its true realm, they had already crossed its borders. Understanding the boy's purpose, the old woman provided him with a piece of meat, a jug filled with milk, and a rope to aid him on his quest. With her words of guidance, she handed him a small bag and vanished into thin air.

Undeterred, the young man pressed on, reaching the mouth of a dark cave. As he entered and proceeded cautiously, the darkness receded, revealing a magnificent house before him. Curiosity piqued, he opened the gate and entered the courtyard, only to be greeted by nine white dogs rushing towards him. Swiftly, he retrieved a piece of meat from his bag, tossing it to the dogs as a gesture of goodwill.

Continuing on, he discovered a well where a woman, using ropes tied to her buckets, tirelessly drew water from its depths. Offering his rope, the young man inquired about her purpose. The woman explained that the water was for washing the bodies of the deceased, whose relatives had neglected this duty. Progressing further, he unlocked the door to a house and found three eggs within. Taking one in his hand, he cracked it open, and a billowing steam emerged, revealing his father who exclaimed, "Oh, I'm hungry and thirsty!" Eagerly, the young man directed his father to the courtyard, where a jug of milk awaited him. Yet, his father expressed gratitude but explained that it was too late for nourishment. He sought only peace before continuing his journey to the realm of the dead. And with those words, he vanished from sight.

Undeterred, the young man opened the second egg and his mother appeared before him, uttering, "Oh, I'm hungry and thirsty." Without hesitation, he directed her to the courtyard, where the jug of milk stood ready for her. Expressing gratitude, his mother acknowledged that it was too late for sustenance but welcomed the opportunity for peace before continuing her path to the realm of death. With those words, she disappeared, leaving the young man with the third and final egg in his grasp.

Filled with anticipation, the young man made his way to the courtyard, where he carefully cracked open the final egg. As its shell broke, a transformation occurred before his eyes. His beloved emerged, radiating beauty like the most enchanting daughter of the sun king. "Oh, I'm hungry and thirsty," she spoke softly. Hastily, he handed her the jug of milk, which she drank, revitalizing her very being. Transformed by the nourishment, she joyfully declared, "My love, you have freed me from the clutches of death. Now, I shall return to the realm of the living and be forever yours."

And so it came to pass. The young couple returned from the treacherous mountain, finding solace in each other's arms. They lived their days in bliss and contentment until the time came for them to embark on their final journey to the realm of the dead. With their love transcending the realms, their spirits found eternal peace and happiness, forever united in the realm beyond life.

And so, in this extraordinary tale of love and redemption, a young Romani boy defied the boundaries of life and death to free his departed loved ones from their restless spirits. Through his unwavering determination and acts of kindness, he found the eggs that held the key to their release, bringing them peace and restoring them to the realm of the living. With their love conquering even the realm of death, they lived in eternal happiness, united forevermore. This enchanting story reminds us that love knows no bounds, and with compassion and selflessness, miracles can unfold, even in the face of darkness and despair.

The Man with Five Heads

Once upon a time, during the joyous Easter season, when the air was filled with anticipation of summer's arrival and the end of winter's grasp, there was a man named Radulj Pista who carried a heavy burden within his heart. While the village came alive with celebrations, Radulj Pista, carrying his trusty anvil and hammer, ventured into the depths of the forest.

There, beneath the towering trees, he kindled a small fire and toiled away tirelessly, shaping one horseshoe after another, and forging nails with his skilled hands. While the villagers gathered in the church, their voices raised in prayer and hymns, Radulj Pista remained focused on his work, unaware of the festivities surrounding him.

Suddenly, a remarkable sight unfolded before him. Emerging from the depths of the woods stood a man with five heads, each one expressing a unique countenance. He approached Radulj Pista, his voice filled with curiosity, and greeted him, "Good day! Are you working even on God's holiday?"

Without hesitation, Radulj Pista replied, "Yes, indeed. For my people at home, I must labor, for without my toil, they would be plagued by hunger and despair."

The man with five heads, showing understanding, responded, "Yet, on this sacred day, it is customary to rest and celebrate. You could choose other days to be more industrious, ensuring your loved ones do not suffer."

An indignant spark ignited within Radulj Pista as he retorted, "It is easy for you to speak such words. You possess five heads, allowing for greater ease of thought, unlike me with only one. In my humble abode, fifteen children dwell, seven of them blind, and seven deaf. As for the youngest, their fate remains uncertain. They depend on me greatly, dear man, and thus I must toil relentlessly to provide for their needs."

The man with five heads paused, a newfound understanding etched across his faces. "I was unaware of your plight," he admitted. "You speak the truth, and your duty is indeed paramount. Even amidst the village's merriment, you should focus on your work. May God bless your endeavors." With those parting words, he departed, vanishing back into the forest.

Meanwhile, at the edge of the village, Radulj Pista's wife sat in their cozy cottage, weaving baskets of various sizes from supple birch branches. She envisioned selling these baskets in the town during the upcoming market day, hoping to bring much-needed provision for their family. Unbeknownst to her, the man with five heads materialized in her presence.

"Good day, dear lady!" he greeted her warmly. "Are you working on God's holiday?"

With a touch of weariness in her voice, she responded,

"Yes, indeed. While my husband forges horseshoes and nails in the fields, I weave these baskets to secure a livelihood for our children. We have seven dear ones who cannot hear and seven precious ones who cannot see."

The man with five heads contemplated her words, his eyes reflecting compassion. "In such circumstances, it is clear you must continue to work," he said gently. "Yet, I wish to alleviate your distress. I possess the power to grant your blind children sight once more and restore hearing to your deaf children. However, in exchange, I must request your youngest child to offer as a sacrifice."

Overwhelmed with sorrow, the poor woman, tears streaming down her face, surrendered her youngest child to the man with five heads. He drew forth a gleaming knife from his belt, performed the solemn sacrifice, and cast the child out of the window onto the street below. With that, the man with five heads vanished into thin air, leaving behind a sense of both relief and anguish within the grieving mother's heart. As her wails of sorrow filled the air, her deaf children, with their acute senses, cried out, "Mother, we hear our little sister crying on the street!"

Startled by their revelation, the seven blind children hurried outside and discovered their youngest sister lying there, miraculously unharmed. With tender care and joyous relief, they lifted her into their arms and brought her back to their mother.

The mother's tears transformed into tears of immense gratitude and happiness as she embraced her complete brood, now reunited and whole. No longer burdened by blindness or deafness, each child possessed the gift of sight and hearing, bestowed upon them through the mysterious sacrifice.

In the village, news of this miraculous event quickly spread, filling the hearts of the villagers with awe and wonder. They marveled at the transformative power of sacrifice and the extraordinary circumstances that had unfolded.

From that day forward, Radulj Pista and his wife, along with their children, lived a life infused with renewed hope and boundless joy. The once burdened family became a beacon of resilience and love, inspiring others with their remarkable tale.

And so, in the enchanting realm of fairy tales, we learn that even in the darkest moments, there is always the possibility of redemption and transformation. Sacrifice, though painful, can bring about unimaginable blessings, illuminating the path toward a future filled with light and happiness.

The Gypsy and The Treasure

Once upon a time, in a land far away, there lived a poor Romani man. He wandered through the forest, carrying the weight of his poverty on his shoulders. Weary and in need of rest, he lay down beneath a mighty tree. As he drifted into a deep slumber, a mysterious lady, clad in a flowing white gown, appeared before him.

The lady approached the sleeping man and spoke with a gentle voice, "I see that you are a poor Romani man, and I wish to bestow wealth upon you. Venture deeper into this enchanted forest, where you will encounter a woman by the river. She holds the key to your prosperity."

As the Romani man awakened, he recalled the lady's words and felt a glimmer of hope ignite within his heart. Determined to improve his circumstances, he delved deeper into the forest, guided by an invisible force. And there, by the shimmering river, stood the woman the lady had mentioned.

With an air of anticipation, the woman greeted him warmly. "Ah, I have been expecting your arrival," she exclaimed. "Follow this river to its source, where an ancient tree stands tall. Beneath its roots lies a treasure destined to be yours. However, heed this advice: when you commence digging, close your eyes tightly and do not open them until a cry reaches your ears."

The Romani man, filled with anticipation, thanked the woman for her guidance. He embarked on his journey, following the meandering river to its very origin. And lo and behold, he found the majestic tree, its branches reaching towards the heavens.

With great determination, the Romani man closed his eyes and began to dig beneath the tree. The earth beneath him seemed to come alive, as if cold serpents slithered across his body, sending shivers down his spine. Yet, he did not waver. He persevered, his trust unwavering, and his eyes remained tightly shut.

As he dug deeper, a searing pain surged through his limbs, as though scalding water cascaded upon his skin. The discomfort was unbearable, and his body trembled uncontrollably, teeth chattering in the cold. Tears welled in his tightly shut eyes, but he resisted the temptation to open them. With unwavering determination, he continued to dig, driven by a promise of unimaginable riches.

Then, from the depths of the earth, a captivating melody reached his ears. Soft arms embraced his weary neck, and warm lips pressed against his own. A voice, both soothing and melodic, whispered, "You have fulfilled your sacred duty, and the treasure is now yours to claim. Come, rest within my embrace."

A surge of excitement coursed through the Romani man's veins, and he almost succumbed to curiosity, tempted to open his eyes. But the words of the mysterious lady echoed in his mind, reminding him of his pledge. With unwavering resolve, he continued to dig, undeterred by the strange occurrences around him.

The ground beneath him began to undulate, rising and falling like waves in a tempestuous sea. He stumbled and swayed, feeling as though he were in a drunken stupor. Then, without warning, a powerful blow struck his head, and he collapsed to the ground. And in that very moment, a piercing cry filled the air.

As the Romani man opened his eyes, he found himself surrounded by an awe-inspiring sight. There were countless baskets that overflowed with shimmering gold, illuminating the forest with their radiant glow. And beside them sat a breathtakingly beautiful girl, a smile adorning her lips. She spoke with a voice filled with gratitude, "You have fulfilled your destined task, and in doing so, you have freed me from my enchantment," she said, her voice filled with gratitude and joy. "Long ago, I lived in this very place where a magnificent house once stood. My days were filled with happiness and contentment, for I lived harmoniously with my dear brother. However, tragedy befell us when my brother fell in love with a married woman. Consumed by his desire, he committed a terrible act, taking her as his own and stealing all the treasures that belonged to her."

The Romani man listened intently, his heart heavy with empathy for the girl's plight. She continued, her voice tinged with sadness, "But their happiness was short-lived. The abundance of wealth corrupted my brother, transforming him into a proud and haughty man. In a fit of rage, his own wife took his life, and then, burdened by remorse, she took her own. As a final act of spite, she cast a curse upon the gold and me. I was transformed into this mighty tree beneath which you dug."

Tears welled in the Romani man's eyes as he realized the depth of the girl's suffering. Determined to bring her peace and fulfill his own destiny, he made a solemn vow to protect and cherish her. Gathering his strength, he returned to the town, procuring wagons to transport the precious treasure. With great care, he loaded the baskets of gold onto the wagons and embarked on the journey back to his home.

Arriving at his humble abode, the Romani man revealed the riches to his community. They marveled at the sight before them, their hearts filled with gratitude for the man who had brought prosperity to their midst. And as for the beautiful girl, she became his beloved wife, their union a testament to love's triumph over adversity.

Together, they lived a life of happiness and contentment, sharing their newfound wealth with those in need. The Romani man's generosity touched the hearts of many, and his name became synonymous with kindness and compassion. And the girl, once trapped in the form of a tree, blossomed alongside her husband, radiating beauty and grace.

Their story echoed through the generations, a tale of perseverance, love, and the transformative power of selflessness. The Romani man's legacy endured, reminding all who heard it of the boundless possibilities that lie within each of us, if only we dare to dream and embark on the journey to fulfill our destinies.

The Seven Brothers and The Devil

Once upon a time, there lived seven brothers with their only sister, a beautiful girl, in a small cottage. The brothers were renowned musicians who played at weddings and baptisms in the surrounding area. Despite their musical talent, they lived in extreme poverty, which saddened them greatly. They longed to see their sister dressed as beautifully as the other ladies in town.

One day, while sitting together in their cottage, they discussed how they could attain wealth when someone knocked on their door. They invited the stranger in, a man cloaked in a wide mantle. The stranger spoke, "I know that you wish to become rich and do not know how to obtain wealth. Well, I can advise you. I will build a magnificent castle overnight and share with you so many treasures that you will become the wealthiest people in the land. But you must promise not to marry off your sister."

The brothers made the promise, and the stranger led them outside the cottage. He pointed to a splendid castle and said, "Behold, the castle is complete, and you can now inhabit it." Then the stranger disappeared, and the seven musicians and their beautiful sister moved into the castle, where they discovered marvelous treasures. A joyful life began as they had plenty of money, and soon good friends gathered around them, enjoying the music and the presence of the beautiful girl.

However, it happened that the lovely maiden fell in love with a man who wished to marry her. The seven brothers pleaded with her not to marry, for it would bring great misfortune upon them all. But she did not listen, and the wedding took place. As everyone in the castle gathered, and the priest bestowed his blessing upon the newlyweds, the stranger entered the room and called aside the seven brothers and the young bride, their sister. He spoke to them, "I built a magnificent castle for you overnight and made you wealthy. However, you did not keep your promise that your sister would not marry. I am the devil, and I will punish you. Your sister will give birth to a goat that will only eat gold and silver! That is your punishment!" And the devil disappeared.

The siblings returned to the guests, but the festivities were over. The thought of the goat spoiled every joy, and they could not find happiness anymore.

Time passed with worry and fear, and the sister of the seven brothers was blessed with pregnancy. On Good Friday, she gave birth to a goat that spoke like a human and immediately started jumping joyfully and playfully around the room. Wherever it found silver and gold objects, it would devour them on the spot. After a few days, there was no gold or silver left in the castle, and the brothers had to gradually sell their horses, oxen, and land just to provide enough gold and silver for the goat. Every day, the goat would remind them, "If you forget even for a single day to give me an abundance of gold and silver, you will see what happens. I will devour all of you and then regurgitate and devour you again, and it will continue until someone rescues me."

Eventually, the brothers noticed that the goat would leave every night and disappear in the darkness. They asked their mother, the goat's mother, if she knew where her son went every night. She replied, "I asked him once, and he butted me in the belly, nearly killing me. I certainly won't ask him again where he goes at night." They also asked their father, the goat's father, if he knew where their son, the goat, went every night. He replied, "Don't even talk to me about that fellow. I asked him once, and he butted me in the back, causing me to lose my sight and hearing. I certainly won't ask him again where he goes at night. If you want to know, go to him, and ask him yourselves. Perhaps he will tell you. But I will tell you this much: If your sister, my wife, gives birth to another goat, I will leave this world and abandon all of you."

The brothers became very saddened and resolved to wait for the goat. When the goat ventured out at night, they followed it and witnessed how it regurgitated and deeply buried all the gold and silver it had consumed during the day. Then they heard the goat speaking to itself, saying, "If my parents and my seven uncles knew where I bury all the gold and silver I eat during the day, they wouldn't be so upset!" When the goat left, the brothers emerged from their hiding place and dug up all the silver and gold from the spot.
They found together all the gold and silver that the goat had ever consumed in its life. They took most of it back home. From that day on, they had no more worries because they only

gave the goat the gold and silver they found in the pit.

After some time, the mother of the goat gave birth to a beautiful girl. Joy and happiness once again filled the castle. Everyone loved the little, graceful girl, especially the goat, who never took his eyes off his sister. They played, cuddled, and watched over her day and night. Only at night would the goat briefly leave to regurgitate and bury the gold and silver he had consumed during the day. The seven brothers would then dig it up again to give it back to him for consumption.

As the little girl grew up into a beautiful maiden, she would spend her days playing with her brother, the goat, in the garden. One day, she overheard her brother, standing behind the garden wall, crying. She also heard him saying to himself, "How happy my little sister is! She is human, and everyone loves her. But as for me, the ugly goat, no one cares. Oh, if she only knew that it is possible to free me and restore my human form, she would surely seek advice from the mist king. But I must not tell her anything, or else the devil would take me to hell, and I would have to serve him as a horse."

When the beautiful girl heard everything and the goat was about to leave, she ran after him and said, "Dear brother, it is a great misfortune that you have the form of a goat. If you were human, I would take you with me on a long journey. You see, I am going to the mist king to seek advice." The goat, surprised, asked his beautiful sister, "What advice does the mist king have for you?" The sister explained, "I had a strange dream. I saw the mist king, who told me to come to his abode, and that he would then tell me how to free you. Tomorrow, I will go to the mist king's dwelling, and when I return, I will free you, and only then will our lives be happy and joyful."

The goat joyfully wagged his tail and said to his sister, "Dear sister, I also have advice for your journey. If you encounter people or animals who try to give you advice, first look at their left foot. If it is covered or even resembles a duck's webbed foot, do not follow their advice, for it is bad and would lead you to ruin."

"I will heed your warning," said the sister, "and today I will embark on my journey."

Then she and her seven uncles went to their parents' house to inform them of her plan.

And so, the maiden set off into the world, wandering for a long time. Along her journey, the maiden encountered various beings and creatures, each offering their guidance and assistance. However, she remembered her brother's advice and carefully examined their left feet. Many of them had covered or webbed feet, indicating that their advice may lead her astray. She politely declined their offers and continued on her path.

As she traveled further, she entered a dense forest, where she stumbled upon a magical spring. The water shimmered with a gentle glow, and a wise old owl perched nearby. The owl greeted her and asked, "Fair maiden, where are you headed on this fine day?" The girl replied, "I seek the counsel of the mist king to free my brother from his goat form."

The owl nodded sagely and said, "I know the way to the mist king's realm, but it is a treacherous journey. However, if you follow me and heed my guidance, I shall lead you safely." The girl glanced at the owl's left foot, and to her relief, it was not covered nor resembled a duck's webbed foot. With a grateful smile, she accepted the owl's guidance.

Through the enchanted forest they ventured, the wise owl leading the way. It warned her of hidden dangers and guided her through the winding paths. After days of travel, they arrived at the mist king's majestic palace, shrouded in a mysterious mist.

Inside the palace, the mist king sat upon his throne, his form barely visible amidst the swirling mist. The girl approached respectfully and shared her tale, expressing her desire to free her brother from the curse. The mist king listened attentively and then spoke in a voice as soft as the mist itself, "To break the curse, you must gather three rare ingredients. The feather of a phoenix, the tear of a mermaid, and the petal of a moonflower."

The girl thanked the mist king for his guidance and set out on her quest to find the three elusive items. With the owl as her companion, she traveled to far-off lands, braving dangerous encounters, and overcoming various obstacles. Through her perseverance and unwavering determination, she succeeded in obtaining the feather of a phoenix, the tear of a mermaid, and the petal of a moonflower.

Returning to the mist king's palace, the girl presented the precious ingredients. The mist king acknowledged her bravery and proclaimed, "With these sacred items, I shall perform the ritual to break the curse." He then conducted an ancient ceremony, invoking powerful magic that filled the air.

As the mist cleared, the goat transformed into a handsome young man, just as he had been before the curse befell him. The girl and her brother embraced, tears of joy streaming down their faces. The mist king, pleased with their triumph, offered them his blessings and guidance for a prosperous future.

Reunited and free from the clutches of the curse, the siblings returned to their castle. The seven brothers rejoiced at the sight of their sister and welcomed their newly restored brother with open arms. The castle once again resonated with music, laughter, and love.

From that day forward, the siblings lived harmoniously, sharing the joys of life and the wealth they had acquired. The beautiful girl found happiness with her true love, and the brothers continued their musical pursuits, filling the castle with melodies that echoed throughout the land.

And so, their tale of resilience, unity, and the triumph of love spread far and wide, inspiring others to believe in the power of family, courage, and the magic that resides within the human spirit.

The Man Without a Shadow

Once upon a time, there were thirteen young Gypsies who made a bold decision to leave their tribe and embark on a journey to explore different cities and encounter new people. For many years, they roamed from town to town and village to village, and fortune smiled upon them as they always found employment.

One fateful day, they stumbled upon a vast desert where no one resided. There was no trace of water, trees, or grass. They wandered through the barren landscape for three days until, on the fourth day, they reached a formidable fortress with imposing iron doors. They knocked on the doors and sought admission. To their surprise, a limping devil emerged and inquired, "What do you seek? Are you hungry and thirsty? Very well, I shall grant you entry and provide you with sustenance and drink." Eagerly, they entered the devil's abode and indulged in a feast, satisfying their hunger, and quenching their thirst.

When the time came to depart, the devil positioned himself at the door and permitted them to leave, save for the last one, whom he detained, declaring, "The last one belongs to me!" The twelve Gypsies found themselves wandering through the desert once again. As starvation loomed, they returned to the devil's dwelling, beseeching him for food and drink. Yet, as they attempted to depart, the same pattern unfolded: the devil claimed the last one. This cycle repeated so frequently that by the eleventh encounter with the devil, only two brothers dared to enter, and only one emerged. The final Gypsy of the original thirteen ventured alone through the vast desert, until eventually, he found himself back in the presence of the limping devil.

Having partaken in another meal and quenched his thirst, the young man expressed his desire to depart. However, the devil declared, "You shall remain here, for someone must stay, and you arrived alone." Unwilling to accept his fate, the young man proposed, "Simply open the door; I have brought one more!" The devil, amused, opened the door and challenged him, saying, "Let me see. You will not escape me!" Standing at the threshold, the young man pointed behind him, directing attention to his own shadow, and declared, "You may keep that one!" Enraged, the devil slammed the door shut. As the young man glanced at his shadow, he discovered that it had vanished.

From that day forward, the Gypsy with no shadow continued his journey through the world. People marveled at his peculiar condition, for it was uncommon to encounter someone without a shadow. His shadowless presence sparked curiosity and whispers wherever he went.

As the Gypsy traveled from town to town, his reputation preceded him. Tales of his enigmatic nature spread far and wide, captivating the imaginations of those who heard. Some believed he possessed magical powers, while others considered him cursed. Regardless, he became a figure of intrigue and wonder.

People would gather in anticipation whenever the shadowless Gypsy arrived in a new place. They sought his counsel and asked for glimpses into their futures. His words held weight, as if the absence of his shadow granted him an unclouded insight into the mysteries of life.

Despite the absence of a shadow, the Gypsy exuded an aura of wisdom and compassion. He would listen attentively to the troubles of others, offering guidance and solace. His presence brought comfort to those burdened by sorrows and hope to those lost in the darkness of uncertainty.

The shadowless Gypsy's path eventually led him to a grand city, where the king had heard tales of his extraordinary existence. Intrigued by the rumors, the king summoned the Gypsy to his palace, eager to experience firsthand the enigma of a man without a shadow.

Upon their meeting, the Gypsy captivated the king with his profound insights and gentle demeanor. The king was deeply moved by the Gypsy's wisdom and asked for guidance on matters of the kingdom. The Gypsy shared his counsel, offering perspectives that the king had never considered.

Impressed by the shadowless Gypsy's wisdom and integrity, the king appointed him as his trusted advisor. The Gypsy served the kingdom with unwavering dedication, using his unique perspective to guide the king through difficult decisions and challenges.

Under the guidance of the shadowless Gypsy, the kingdom flourished. Prosperity and harmony filled the land, and the people admired the wise counsel of their shadowless advisor. The king valued the Gypsy's insights above all else, recognizing the extraordinary gift he possessed.

As the years passed, the shadowless Gypsy's reputation spread beyond the kingdom's borders. Rulers from distant lands sought his guidance and sent emissaries to request his presence in their courts. The Gypsy's influence extended far and wide, bridging gaps between kingdoms and fostering a spirit of unity.

Despite the honor and respect he received, the shadowless Gypsy remained humble and grounded. He never forgot his roots as one of the thirteen adventurous Gypsies who had set out into the world. He continued to offer his wisdom and guidance, inspiring others to embrace their unique qualities and seek enlightenment within themselves.

And so, the shadowless Gypsy's story became a legend, a tale passed down through generations. He became a symbol of resilience, reminding people that even in the absence of something ordinary, there lies the potential for extraordinary wisdom and inner light.

Nothingness

Once upon a time, in a village, there lived a man who was very poor. He worked only enough to avoid starvation, but he was known among the people as a wise man and a true jack-of-all-trades. He excelled in every craft he tried, whether it was blacksmithing, carpentry, or tailoring. However, he only worked until he earned a few coins to buy himself food. After satisfying his hunger, he would return to his large and beautiful house, which remained empty as its owner acquired nothing and lived day by day.

One fateful day, while the man was dozing off in his home, a fat and naked man entered the room. The stranger approached the man and declared, "You are my best companion. You have nothing, and I have nothing. You need nothing, and I need nothing. Besides, my name is 'Nothing.' I like it here, and I will live here." As the man scrutinized the stranger, he realized that the visitor was as transparent as window glass. He responded, "If you have no need for food or drink, you can stay with me forever. However, I won't provide you with any provisions." The stranger reiterated, "I already told you that I have nothing and need nothing. And it seems that you have nothing too, otherwise I wouldn't have come to you. I seek refuge only with those who have nothing and need nothing because I am Nothing." With that, the stranger made himself comfortable in the empty room and lay down.

The man continued with his usual work routine. Once he earned a few coins, he would eat his fill and then retire to his humble abode for rest. This pattern persisted for some time until the man noticed that Mr. Nothing was gradually growing fatter with each passing day. Before long, the stranger occupied almost the entire room, leaving little space for the host. Frustrated by the situation, the man confronted Mr. Nothing and said, "Listen, my friend! You are expanding more and more each day, and soon there will be no room left in my house for me to lay down." Mr. Nothing let out a yawn and responded, "I can't help it! It doesn't concern me!" As time went on, Mr. Nothing grew so large that the man could barely stand in the room, let alone sit or lie down.

Then, the man fell in love with a beautiful girl and desired to marry her. However, the girl's parents had one condition. They admired the man's skills and knowledge in various crafts but insisted that he acquire possessions. They pointed out that his room, stable, cellar, and attic were all empty. They urged him to gather what was necessary, and only then would they grant him permission to marry their daughter. Motivated by love, the man began working diligently day and night. He labored tirelessly, gradually acquiring household tools, clothing, livestock, and everything else he needed. As his collection of possessions grew, Mr. Nothing started shrinking in size until he settled in a corner near the stove.

Once the man had filled every empty space in his house, cellar, attic, and barn, he approached the girl's parents and obtained their consent to marry their daughter. On the day of the wedding, as the man entered the room with his young wife, he noticed that Mr. Nothing was nowhere to be found. The stranger had moved on to someone else, having fulfilled his purpose.

And so, the man and his wife lived happily in their home, filled with the fruits of their hard work and love. They enjoyed the comfort and security that their possessions provided, but they also cherished the knowledge that true happiness came from within and not from material things.

As the years went by, the man continued to use his skills and knowledge to bring prosperity to their household. He became renowned in the village as a successful craftsman, creating beautiful works of art and providing for his family's needs.

One day, a traveler passing through the village heard of the man's talents and sought him out. The traveler was in search of someone who could create a special gift for a distant king. Impressed by the man's craftsmanship, the traveler commissioned him to make a unique and extraordinary piece.

Excited by the opportunity, the man poured his heart and soul into the creation. He worked tirelessly, pushing the boundaries of his abilities, and the result was a masterpiece beyond compare. The traveler was astounded by the man's skill and promised to deliver the gift to the king personally.

Months later, news arrived that the king was overjoyed with the gift. He was so impressed by the man's talent that he invited him to the royal palace. The man, accompanied by his wife, embarked on a journey to the grand castle, where they were welcomed with honor and respect.

In the palace, they were surrounded by opulence and splendor, but they never forgot their humble beginnings. They remained humble and grateful for the opportunities life had bestowed upon them.

During their stay, the man had the chance to meet other skilled craftsmen from all over the kingdom. They exchanged ideas, techniques, and stories, further enriching his own knowledge and inspiring him to reach new heights.

When it was time to return home, the man and his wife carried with them memories of a grand adventure and a renewed sense of purpose. They continued their life together, using their wealth and influence to help those in need and promote the value of hard work and perseverance.

Their story spread far and wide, becoming a legend that inspired others to pursue their passions and appreciate the true treasures in life. The man's legacy lived on, not only through his masterful creations but also through the values he instilled in his children and the generations to come.

And so, the man and his wife lived a life filled with love, happiness, and fulfillment, proving that true wealth lies not in possessions alone but in the joy found in following one's passion and sharing that joy with others.

Conclusion

In closing, *Don't Call Me Gypsy* invites us to reflect upon the profound journey we have undertaken, exploring the intricate tapestry of the Romani community's history, culture, and identity. Throughout these pages, we have embarked on a transformative voyage of understanding, encountering the challenges, triumphs, and resilient spirit of the Romani people.

Our exploration began with an exploration of the Romani presence in the Czech Lands, unearthing the threads that connect them to the broader societal fabric. We navigated the nomadic lifestyle, witnessing the beauty and complexities of a culture shaped by constant movement and adaptation.

As we ventured further, we encountered the shadows cast by historical events, delving into the impact of World War II and the Nazis on the Romani community. Through these narratives, we bore witness to the indomitable spirit that defied oppression and preserved the Romani identity against all odds. We explored the facets of Romani nationality, delving into the intricate layers of lifestyle, traditions, and spirituality that shape their collective consciousness.

From the resounding beats of Romani music and the rhythmic movements of dance, to the enchanting world of the circus and the transformative power of theater, we discovered the vibrant cultural expressions that breathe life into the Romani heritage. We delved into the richness of Romani language and oral tradition, unraveling the enchanting fairytales that have been passed down through generations, weaving lessons of resilience, morality, and the human experience.

As we draw the final curtain, let this bhook serve as an enduring testament to the enduring strength, resilience, and cultural contributions of the Romani community. May this exploration foster empathy, understanding, and appreciation for their rich tapestry of traditions and serve as a catalyst for positive change. Let us carry the knowledge and insights gained from these pages, honoring the Romani people's legacy by working towards a future where inclusivity, respect, and cultural celebration form the foundation of our society.

About the Author

 Kytka Hilmarová, a Prague native and political refugee, embarked on a transformative journey at a young age when she and her parents' sought asylum in the United States in 1968. As an accomplished author, translator, and publisher, Hilmarová has left an indelible mark on the literary world, bridging the gap between Czech literature and English-speaking readers.

With over 200 books brought to life as a prolific ghostwriter and a portfolio of translating more than 100 Czech literary works into English, Hilmarová acts as a vital bridge connecting Czech literature with a global audience. Her visionary approach and unwavering commitment to preserving and promoting Czech culture, history, tradition, and literature have ensured that the legacy of Czech literary works remains alive, vibrant, and cherished for generations to come.

As the founder of Czech Revival Publishing, Hilmarová showcases the rich tapestry of Czech literary gems, fostering cultural exchange and expanding the global reach of Czech authors. Through her captivating works and translations, she invites readers to immerse themselves in the enchanting world of Czech literature, offering a glimpse into its diverse themes, profound emotions, and timeless wisdom.

Join Kytka Hilmarová on a literary journey that illuminates the treasures of Czech literature, history, and tradition. Her exceptional talent, resilience, and relentless pursuit of bridging cultures make her an indispensable figure in bringing the richness of Czech literature to English-speaking audiences, ensuring its enduring legacy for years to come.

10% of book proceeds support the preservation of Czech culture in the United States. Learn more about our efforts to safeguard and enhance Czech traditions, language, arts, and history through the following:

Czechs in America Organization (CIAO) is dedicated to fostering the appreciation, understanding, and teaching of Czech culture and history. We exist to preserve, promote, and support efforts to perpetuate the Czech culture, history, customs, and traditions in the United States.
CzechAmerica.org

The Czech Museum has been established with the purpose of preserving, collecting, exhibiting, researching, and interpreting a collection of artifacts and archival material related to Czech history and culture.
TheCzechMuseum.org

Everything Czech is dedicated to fostering a profound understanding and appreciation of the unique and vibrant history, culture, and traditions of the Czech people.
EverythingCzech.com

Made in the USA
Las Vegas, NV
19 July 2023